Easy *Arabic* Reader

Easy *Arabic* Reader

A Three-Part Text for Beginning Students

Mahmoud Gaafar & Jane Wightwick

New York Chicago San Francisco Lisbon London Madrid Mexico City
Milan New Delhi San Juan Seoul Singapore Sydney Toronto

The **McGraw-Hill** Companies

1 2 3 4 5 6 7 8 9 10 11 12 13 14 15 16 QFR/QFR 1 9 8 7 6 5 4 3 2 1

ISBN 978-0-07-175402-6
MHID 0-07-175402-4

Library of Congress Cataloging-in-Publication Data

Gaafar, Mahmoud.
Easy Arabic reader : a three-part text for beginning students / Mahmoud Gaafar and Jane Wightwick.
p. cm. — (Easy reader series)
ISBN 978-0-07-175402-6 (alk. paper)
1. Arabic language—Readers. I. Wightwick, Jane. II. Title.

PJ6119.G23 2011
492.7—dc22 2011006124

The author would like to thank the following for permission to reproduce images: background pattern, © iStockphoto.com/Petra Mezei; page 13, © iStockphoto .com/Huseyin Turgut Erkisi; page 15, © iStockphoto.com/Evan Meyer; page 19, © iStockphoto.com/Royce DeGrie; page 23, © Bangin; page 25, © iStockphoto.com/ Rilueda; page 29, © iStockphoto.com/Atbaei; page 33, © iStockphoto.com/Atbaei; page 34, © Durbaquista; page 39, © iStockphoto.com/Joel Carillet; page 43, © Ranveig Thattai; page 45, © iStockphoto.com/David Bjorgen; page 47, © iStockphoto.com/ David Kerkhoff; page 53, © iStockphoto.com/Danijela Pavlovic Markovic; page 54, © iStockphoto.com/Lars Kirchhoff; page 57, © iStockphoto.com/Martti Salmela; page 59, © iStockphoto.com/Szilvia Gogh; page 61, © iStockphoto.com/Joel Carillet; page 69, © Al Musawwir; page 73, © PD-ART; page 77, © Al Musawwir; page 79, © Blago Tebi; page 83, © M. Waguaf; page 85, The Yorck Project; page 89, © Dar al-Hayat

This book is printed on acid-free paper.

Bonus audio recordings online!

Perfect your Arabic pronunciation by listening to audio recordings of the reading passages from all forty-one chapters of the book. Spoken by native Arabic speakers, the recordings are conveniently arranged for quick and easy access.

Go to www.audiostudyplayer.com, launch the Study Player, and then select:

Arabic › Easy Arabic Reader › Part 1: Jamal's Journey, etc.

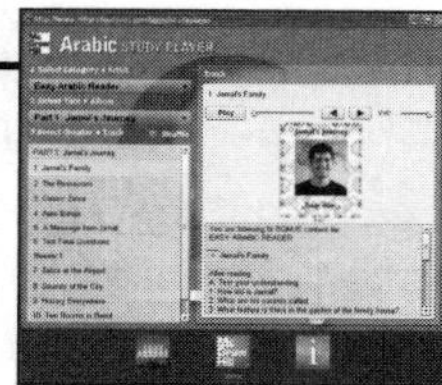

Contents المُحتَويات

Part Two: Arab Characters
الجُزء الثاني: شَخصيّات عَرَبيّة

Part Three: Ali Baba and the Forty Thieves

الجُزء الثالث: علي بابا والأربعين حرامي

(A modern interpretation)

Introduction المُقَدّمة

Easy Arabic Reader has been designed to provide learners of Arabic with a bridge between textbooks and authentic material. Articles, blogs, stories, and novels written for native Arabic speakers can be challenging, except perhaps for more advanced students. On the other hand, material written for young Arab children learning to read is not always suitable for older learners of Arabic as a foreign or second language.

Easy Arabic Reader can be used by learners studying independently or in a group and is suitable for a wide range of abilities. Beginning students will need a basic knowledge of the Arabic language and script but will then find the material accessible if they follow the strategies recommended in this Introduction. Intermediate and advanced students can plot their own course through the book, concentrating on texts and language of particular interest.

Arabic has a long tradition of storytelling. Developing a feel for Arabic through stories will improve your understanding of the language, as well as help you appreciate the rythmn and style. *Easy Arabic Reader* will also help you to develop skills such as reading for gist or for specific information and guessing vocabulary in context or by connection to other familiar words.

Easy Arabic Reader provides every learner of Arabic with a wealth of lively material written in simplified Modern Standard Arabic, together with illuminating explanatory notes, comprehension exercises, and a variety of activities designed to aid understanding and vocabulary retention. Our aim is to help learners of Arabic develop their knowledge of Modern Standard Arabic, while at the same time reading stories that are genuinely enjoyable and original in their own right.

There are three parts to the text, and there is a basic progression in terms of language level through the parts. However, this progression is not as strict as in a more formal course, and it is not absolutely necessary to read the parts in the order they are presented. For a beginning student, however, we recommend reading the texts sequentially and completing the activities based on the texts. (It is also possible to read the English comprehension questions *before* the Arabic text for additional help in anticipating the content.)

Part One is the ficticious account of an Arab American college student, Jamal, who lives in California with his family. Jamal goes on his first trip to visit his relatives in Syria and to travel around the Middle East. Through his impressions of his visit and his travels through the different countries, we come to know more about life and popular culture in the Arab world.

Part Two consists of five minibiographies of prominent figures in Arabic history and culture. The personalities are carefully chosen to reflect a range of different fields and eras in Arabic history.

Part Three is a contemporary take on a traditional story from *One Thousand and One Nights*: *Ali Baba and the Forty Thieves*. This has been written and illustrated especially for *Easy Arabic Reader* by Mahmoud Gaafar. The story, illustrations, and copious notes will help clarify the vocabulary and any concepts you may find unfamiliar.

A very important advantage to *Easy Arabic Reader* is the linked audio available online at **www.audiostudyplayer.com**. The lively recordings not only help bring the stories to life, but also make the material far more accessible to lower-level learners who are still struggling with reading Arabic text fluently. After you have listened a few times to a passage while following the text, you will find you are more equipped to re-read the passages in detail by yourself.

We have included in the text the short Arabic vowels that are essential for reading, especially when vocabulary is first encountered. However, if a word is very common or is repeated more than once or twice in the same section, the short vowels are dropped to encourage you to learn to recognize them. This way you will be more prepared to read authentic material, most of which does not display any of the short vowels because the reader is expected to know them. We have also made a conscious decision to generally not include the higher-level, more formal grammatical endings that are sometimes seen in Arabic reading material for learners. The grammatical endings are not necessary for understanding and can add an extra barrier that affects the naturalness of the language and make these types of stories less accessible.

Easy Arabic Reader is an entertaining way of learning about the Arabic language, culture, and history while improving your understanding and fluency in reading. *Easy Arabic Reader* can continue to be a source of learning and amusement as your language level improves. Every time you pick it up to re-read a section, you will probably discover a new twist, angle, or expression that will enrich your grasp of Arabic.

Part One

الجزء الأوّل

Jamal's Journey

رِحلة جمال

Jamal's Family عائِلة جمال

يَعيش جَمال (٢٢) مع أَبيه عَدنان وأُمّه بَسمة في مدينة مونتيري (Monterey) بِشَمال وِلاية كاليفورنيا.

بَيتهُم مُتَوَسِّط الحَجم. الحَديقة واسِعة وفيها حَمّام سِباحة صَغير، وهُناك شُرفة كَبيرة تُطِلّ على المُحيط الهادئ.

جمال يُحِبّ التَصوير، وعلى الحَوائِط في حُجرته هناك صُوَر لِمَعالِم كاليفورنيا مِثل الجُسور في سان فرانسيسكو، والشاطِئ والميناء في مونتيري، وقَلعة «راندولف هيرست».

جمال يَدرُس هَندَسة المِعمار، وهو يَرى أن التصوير يُساعِده كَثيراً في دِراسته. فَوقَ مَكتَب جمال هناك صورة قديمة لِلمُمَثِّل «كلينت ايستوود» مَكتوب عليها تحيّة بِخَطّ يَده.

مَعَ أبيه *with his father*
وِلاية *state*
مُتَوَسِّط الحَجم *medium-sized*
شُرفة *balcony*
تُطِلّ على *overlooking*
المُحيط الهادِئ *Pacific Ocean*
التَصوير *photography*
حَوائِط *walls*
مَعالِم *landmarks*
شاطِئ *beach*
ميناء *port*
قلعة *castle/fort*
هَندَسة المِعمار *architecture*
يَرى *[he] thinks/sees*
يُساعِده *helps him*
مُمَثّل *actor*
تَحيّة *greeting*
خَطّ يَده *his handwriting*

After reading بَعدَ القِراءة

A **Test your understanding.**

1 How old is Jamal?
2 What are his parents' names?
3 What feature is there in the garden of the family house?
4 What does Jamal have on the walls of his room?
5 What does Jamal study?
6 Whose signed photo hangs above Jamal's desk?

B **Match the Arabic expressions from the reading passage to the English equivalents.**

a California landmarks	١ بخطّ يده
b he thinks that	٢ مَعالِم كاليفورنيا
c Randolph Hearst Castle	٣ هو يرى أن
d in the north of…	٤ الجُسور في سان فرانسيسكو
e in his handwriting	٥ بشمال
f the bridges in San Francisco	٦ قَلعة «راندولف هيرست»

قَلعة «راندولف هيرست»، كاليفورنيا

The Restaurant المَطعَم

يَملِك عدنان مَطعَماً في مدينة كارميل (Carmel) القَريبة من بيتهم يُقدِّم فيه المَأكولات الشَّرقِيّة اللَذيذة. المطعم مَفتوح طَوال الأُسبوع، ولكِنّ عدنان يَعمَل فيه من يَوم الثُلاثاء إلى الأحَد فَقَط. هو لا يَذهَب إلى المطعم يوم الاِثنَين ويَترُك كُلّ شَيء في رِعاية كارلوس، الطَّبّاخ المَكسيكيّ. عدنان يَلعَب التَنِس أو يَصطاد السَّمَك مع أَصدِقاءه في يوم العُطلة.

أَمّا بسمة فَهي تُساعِد عدنان في شِراء الفَواكِه والخُضار والسمك، ولكن هِواياتها هي الموسيقى وتَعَلُّم اللُّغات. بسمة تَتَحَدَّث العَرَبيّة والفَرَنسيّة والإيطاليّة، وتَتَحَدَّث الإسبانيّة مع كارلوس، وأَيضاً تُدَرِّس اللُغة العربيّة للأطفال.

يساعد جمال أباه في المطعم في شُهور الصَيف. جمال يُرَحِّب بالنُقود التي يَكسِبها لأَنَّه سَيَحتاجها في رِحلته إلى الشَرق الأَوسَط لزِيارة خالَته وأولادها.

يَملِك *[he] owns*
يُقَدِّم *he serves*
مأكولات لَذيذة *delicious dishes*
طَوال *throughout*
يَترُك *he leaves*
في رِعاية *in the care of*
يَصطاد السَّمك *he goes fishing*
يَوم العُطلة *the day off*
شراء *buying*
فواكه *fruit(s)*
خُضار *vegetables*
هِواياتها *her hobbies*
تَعلّم اللُغات *learning languages*
تَتَحَدَّث *[she] speaks/talks*
تُدَرِّس *[she] teaches*
شُهور *months*
يُرَحِّب بـ... *welcomes*
نُقود *cash*
يَكسبها *he earns [it]*
سَيَحتاجها *he will need it*
الشَّرق الأوسَط *the Middle East*

After reading بعد القراءة

A Test your understanding.

1 How many days a week is the restaurant open?
2 Which day is Adnan's day off?
3 What does Adnan like doing on his day off?
4 Who is Carlos?
5 How does Basma help out in the restaurant?
6 What are her hobbies?
7 When does Jamal help out in the restaurant?
8 Who is Jamal planning to visit on his trip to the Middle East?

B The expression أما... فَـ... (as for... then...) is a stylistic device used to change subject. Look at the example below from the text, then see if you can rephrase the other sentences in the same way.

بسمة تُساعد عدنان. ← أمّا بسمة فهي تُساعد عدنان.

Basma helps Adnan. → As for Basma, [then] she helps Adnan.

١ بسمة تَتكَلّم الفرنسيّة.

٢ عدنان يلعب التنس.

٣ جمال يُرَحّب بالنُقود.

٤ يساعد جمال أباه في المطعم.

٥ تُدَرِّس بسمة اللُغة العربيّة للأطفال.

٦ لا يذهب عدنان إلى المطعم يوم الاثنين.

Cousin Zahra زهرة، اِبنة الخالة

تعيش زَهرة (٢٤) مع أمّها بَهيجة وأخيها فادي في شقّة كبيرة في مدينة دِمَشق. بهيجة هي أُخت بسمة، أَيّ أَنَّها خالة جمال.

شَقّة *apartment*
أيّ أن *meaning that*

سَقف الشقّة عالٍ لأنّها في بِناية قَديمة. الشقّة فيها حُجرات كَثيرة واسِعة، مِنها حُجرة يَستَخدِمونَها لِتَخزين الحَقائِب ودَرّاجة فادي وبَعض الصَناديق الخَشَبيّة وبيانو أَسوَد عَتيق لَهُ ثَلاث أَرجُل.

سَقف *ceiling*
بِناية *building*
واسِع *spacious*
يُستَخدِمونَها *[that] they use*
لِتَخزين *for storage*
صَناديق خَشَبيّة *wooden boxes*
عَتيق *ancient*
أرجُل *legs*

تَخَرَّجَت زهرة من مَدرَسة التَمريض وتعمل الآن كَمُديرة لعِيادة طَبيب أَسنان سوريّ مَشهور اِسمه دُكتور صَفوان حَلَبيّ. الدكتور يُحِبّ زهرة كَابِنَته، لأنّه كان صَديقاً لأبيها الذي ماتَ في الحَرب.

تَخَرَّجَت *[she] graduated*
مَدرَسة التَمريض *nursing school*
كَمُديرة *as a manager*
عِيادة *clinic/practice*
كَابِنَتِه *as his daughter*
ماتَ *[he] died*
حَرب *war*

تعمل زهرة في العيادة من الخامِسة بَعدَ الظُهر وحَتّى العاشِرة والنِصف مَساءً من السَبت إلى الأربِعاء. هذه المَواعيد تُناسِب زهرة لأنّها تساعد أمّها فى أعمال المَنزِل في الصَباح.

وحَتّى *until*
مَواعيد *hours/times*
تُناسِب *suit*
أعمال المَنزِل *housework*

After reading بعد القراءة

A Test your understanding.

1 Where does Zahra live?
2 Whom does she live with?
3 What relation is Zahra's mother to Jamal's mother, Basma?
4 What four things are mentioned as being kept in the storage room?
5 What is Zahra's profession?
6 Who is Dr. Safwan Halabi?
7 What hours does Zahra work?
8 What does she do in the mornings?

B Decide if these Arabic sentences about the text are true or false.

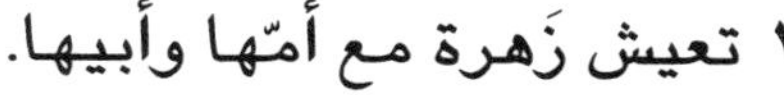

١ تعيش زَهرة مع أمّها وأبيها.

٢ تعيش زَهرة في سوريا.

٣ أمّ زهرة اسمها بهيجة.

٤ بهيجة هي أُخت جمال.

٥ شقّتهم صغيرة.

٦ البيانو له أربع أرجُل.

٧ تعمل زهرة كَطبيبة أسنان.

٨ تعمل بهيجة خمسة أيام في الأُسبوع.

٩ تساعد زهرة أمّها مساءً.

١٠ مات أبو زهرة في الحرب.

بيانو أسود عَتيق

Aunt Bahija الخالة بهيجة

الخالة بهيجة تُحِبّ الاِستِماع إلى الموسيقى، وكانَت تَعزِف على البيانو وهي طِفلة. أمّا الآن فهي تُحاوِل أن تَتَعَلَّم مَهارات الكومبيوتر، ويُساعدها فادي. أكثَر ما يُعجِبها في الكومبيوتر هو أنّها تَستَطيع أن تَتَحَدَّث مع أُختها بسمة في كاليفورنيا وتَراها على الشاشة في نَفس الوَقت. في بَعض الأَعياد تَستَغرِق المُكالَمة أكثر من ساعة!

بهيجة كانَت ماهِرة في أعمال المَنزِل، وكانت مَعروفة في الأسرة بِطبخ المَأكولات السوريّة اللَذيذة. ولكن في السَنَوات القَليلة الماضِية تُعاني بهيجة من بعض المَشاكِل الصِحّيّة بِسَبَب وَزنها الزائِد.

والآن، فَإنّ زهرة هي التي تَقوم بِكُلّ أعمال المنزل. بهيجة فَخورة بِابنَتها لأنّها عَلَّمَتها كلّ المهارات التي تَحتاجها.

الاِستِماع إلى *listening to*
كانَت تَعزِف على *she used to play*
تُحاوِل *[she] tries*
مَهارات *skills*
ما يُعجِبها *what pleases her*
تَستَطيع أن *[she] can/is able to*
تَراها *see her*
شاشة *screen*
أعياد *holidays (Eids)*
تَستَغرِق *lasts*
مُكالَمة *[phone] conversation*
ماهِرة *skillful*
الأُسرة *the family*
طَبخ *cooking*
تُعاني من *[she] suffers from*
مَشاكِل صِحّيّة *health problems*
وَزنها الزائِد *her excessive weight*
تَقوم بـ... *[she] undertakes*
فَخورة بـ... *proud of*
عَلَّمَتها *she taught her*

After reading بعد القراءة

A Test your understanding.

1 When she was a child, Bahija used to play…
 a the guitar. b the flute. c the piano.

2 She is trying to learn skills on…
 a the piano. b the computer. c the cell phone.

3 Bahija likes the computer because she can…
 a talk to her sister on it. b play games on it. c plan her holidays on it.

4 On some holidays, Bahija talks to Basma for…
 a half an hour. b a few minutes. c more than an hour.

5 Bahija taught Zahra how to…
 a cook. b use the computer. c play the piano.

6 Bahija suffers from health problems because of…
 a suffering from a backache. b being overweight. c smoking.

B Match the two halves of the sentences.

١ علّمت بهيجة ابنتها...	ا ...مهارات الكومبيوتر.
٢ تستغرق المكالمة...	ب ...بطبخ المأكولات السوريّة.
٣ أكثر ما يعجب بهيجة هو...	ت ...على البيانو.
٤ بهيجة تعاني من...	ث ...أعمال المنزل.
٥ كانت بهيجة تعزف...	ج ...أنّها ترى أختها على الشاشة.
٦ فادي يعلّم أمّه...	ح ...بعض المشاكل الصحّيّة.
٧ بهيجة كانت معروفة...	خ ...إلى الموسيقى
٨ بهيجة تحبّ الاِستِماع...	د ...أكثر من ساعة.

A Message from Jamal رِسالة من جمال

عَزيزتي زهرة،

كَيف حالكُم؟ كَيف صِحّة خالتي بهيجة؟ وكَيف حال فادي؟ هل لا يَزال أذكى شابّ في كلّ دمشق؟ أنا لا أستَطيع الاِنتِظار حَتّى يَأتي ميعاد سَفَري إلَيكم يوم الخَميس القادِم.

أرَدتُ أن أؤَكِد مَوعِد وُصولي مَرّة أُخرى: أنا سَأُغادِر سان فرانسيسكو يوم الخَميس بعد الظهر وأَصِل لُندُن يوم الجُمعة ظهراً. بعد حَوالي خمس ساعات في المَطار سَآخُذ الخُطوط الجَويّة السوريّة من لندن إلى دمشق. سَأكون مَعكم حوالي الساعة الثالِثة صَباحاً يوم السبت.

أنا أُحاوِل أن أَجمَع أكبَر كَمّيّة مُمكِنة من الدولارات لأنّني أُريد أن أقضي يوليو وأُغسطس معكم. أتَمَنّى أن أَزور لُبنان والأُردُنّ ومِصر أيضاً – وهذا سَيَحتاج إلى كَمّيّة لا بَأس بِها من الدولارات.

ماما تَنوي أن تَزوركُم في العام القادِم. أمّا بابا فَهو لا يَستَطيع أن يَترُك المطعم لِفَترة طويلة.

اِبن خالتك، جمال.

لا يَزال... *he is still...*	خُطوط جَويّة *airline*
أذكَى *smartest/cleverest*	أَجمَع *[I] gather/collect together*
شابّ *youth/young person*	كَمّيّة *quantity*
الاِنتِظار *wait(ing)*	أقضي *[I] stay/spend time*
ميعاد *time/appointment*	أتَمَنّى أن أزور *I hope to visit*
أرَدتُ أن أُوَكِد *I wanted to confirm*	لا بأس بِها *fairly large/not inconsiderable*
مَوعِد وُصول *arrival time*	تَنوي *[she] intends*
سَأُغادِر *I will leave*	يترُك *[he] leaves (behind)*
حَوالي *approximately*	فترة *period (of time)*

الخُطوط الجَويّة السوريّة

After reading بعد القراءة

A Test your understanding.

1 What is the Arabic equivalent of the English opening "*Dear...*"?
2 When is Jamal leaving California for his trip?
3 Is he travelling to Syria on a direct flight?
4 How long does he want to spend in the Middle East?
5 What other countries does he hope to visit?
6 When does Jamal's mother, Basma, hope to visit Damascus?
7 Will his father, Adnan, travel with her? Why/why not?

B Fill out this table with Jamal's flight itinerary.

City	Arrival	Departure
San Francisco	X	
	Friday noon	
Damascus		X

6 Two Final Questions سُؤالان أَخيران

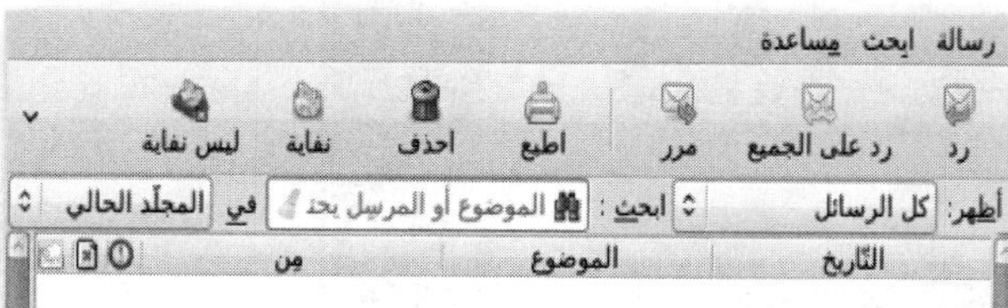

زهرة، عِندي سُؤالان قَبلَ وُصولي...

أَوّلاً: أبي حَذَّرَني من التصوير فوق الجُسور، أو داخِل المَطارات، أو أمامَ المَباني الحُكوميّة. هل هو يُبالِغ؟ في الحَقيقة أنا أنوي أن أُصَوِّر الأماكِن الأَثَريّة فقط وخاصّةً المَساجِد والقُصور. أمّي قالَت إنّني لَو وَجَدتُ نَفسي في مَوقِف شائِك مع الشُرطة فَيَجِب أن أَتَذَكَّر ثلاثة أشياء، وهي الصَبر والأَدَب والاِبتِسام. قالَت إن هذه الصِفات الثلاث سَتَحِلّ أَعقَد المشاكِل. أمّي حَذَّرَتني أيضاً من الصِّياح لأنّه يُعَقِّد الأُمور.

ثانِياً: لي صَديق هُنا اِسمه دانيال وهو نِصف يونانيّ ونصف مِصريّ من الإسكَندَريّة. طَلَبَ مِني دانيال أن أَشتَري لَهُ لُعبة طاوِلة الزَّهر بالصَّدَف. أَعتَقِد أن هذه الحِرفة اليَدَوِيّة مَشهورة عِندَكُم في سوريا. ما هو أَفضَل مَكان لِشِراء واحِدة؟

إلى اللِقاء... جمال

سُؤالان	*two questions*
حَذَّرَني	*[he] warned me*
المَباني	*buildings*
يُبالِغ	*[he] exaggerates*
أماكِن أثَريّة	*archeological sites*
مَوقِف شائِك	*thorny situation*
يَجِب أن أَتَذَكَّر	*I should remember*
اِبتِسام	*smiling*
أعقَد المَشاكِل	*trickiest problems*
صِياح	*shouting*
يُعَقِّد الأُمور	*complicates matters*
يونانيّ	*Greek*
طاوِلة الزَّهر	*backgammon set*
صَدَف	*mother-of-pearl*
حرفة يَدَوِيّة	*handicraft*
لِشِراء	*(in order) to buy*

After reading بعد القراءة

A Test your understanding.

1 Jamal's father has warned him about…

a visiting sites. b taking photos. c going to the airport.

2 Jamal intends to take photos mainly of…

a government buildings. b airports and bridges. c mosques and castles.

3 Jamal is asking Zahra if…

a she can talk to his father. b she agrees with his father's warning.

c she can take pictures for him.

4 When dealing with the police, Jamal's mother recommends…

a manners, smiling, confidence. b patience, manners, smiling.

c shouting, patience, smiling.

5 Jamal's friend Daniel has mixed parentage from…

a Greece and Egypt. b Greece and Syria. c Greece and Turkey.

6 Daniel wants Jamal to bring him…

a a handmade backgammon set.

b details of the best place to buy backgammon sets.

c a photo of people playing backgammon.

طاولة الزهر بالصَّدَف

Review 1

المراجعة ١

تَعيش بسمة مع عائِلَتها الصغيرة في كاليفورنيا. زَوجها عدنان يَملِك مطعماً لِلمأكولات الشَرقيّة في مدينة كارميل القريبة من بيتهم. اِبنها جمال يَدرُس الهَندَسة، ويُساعِد أبيه في المطعم في شُهور الصَّيف. يُريد جمال أن يُسافِر إلى الشَّرق الأَوسَط لِزيارة خالته بهيجة وأولادها زهرة وفادي الذين يعيشون في سوريا. يَتَمَنَّى جمال أن يزور لُبنان والأُردُنّ ومِصر أيضاً. رِحلة الطيران من سان فرانسيسكو إلى دمشق سَتكون طويلة وصَعبة، ولكن جمال لا يَستَطيع الاِنتِظار حتّى يَأتي مَوعِد سَفَره!

شقّة بهيجة في دمشق كبيرة وواسِعة وفيها حُجرات كثيرة. سَقفها عالٍ لأنّها في بِناية قديمة. هناك حُجرة يَستَخدِمونَها لِتَخزين الحَقائِب ودَرّاجة فادي وبَعض الصَناديق الخَشَبيّة وبيانو أسوَد عَتيق لَهُ ثلاث أرجُل.

بهيجة أُخت بسمة ماهِرة في أعمال المَنزِل، وكانَت معروفة في الأسرة بِطبخ المأكولات السوريّة اللذيذة وبِأَنّها تحبّ الاِستِماع إلى الموسيقى. اِبنَتها زهرة تَعمَل كَمُديرة لِعِيادة طبيب أسنان سوريّ مَشهور وابنها فادي يُحاوِل أن يُعَلِّمها مَهارات الكمبيوتر.

Vocabulary review مُراجَعة المُفرَدات

Across

1 حُجرة (4)

7 رِحلة (7)

8 أعمال المَنزِل (9)

9 الشَّرق الأوسَط (3,6,4)

11 مَهارات (6)

12 عائِلة (6)

13 زوج (7)

Down

1 مَطعَم (10)

2 يَعيشون (4,4)

3 بِيانو (5)

4 شَقّة (9)

5 صَناديق (5)

6 يَدرُس (2,7)

10 تُساعِد (هي) (3,5)

Zahra at the Airport زهرة في المطار

وَصَلَت زهرة إلى المَطار قَبلَ مَوعد الطائِرة بِساعة. تَجَوَّلَت داخِل قاعة الوُصول وقَرَأَت الإِعلانات كُلّها: العُطور والمَشروبات وشَركات تَأجير السَّيّارات والخُطوط الجَويّة.

ثُمَّ جلَسَت تُراقِب الناس وتَتَخَيَّل قِصَصهم. هذه السيِّدة رُبَّما جاءَت لِتَستقبِل زَوجها. وهذا الشابّ رُبَّما يَنتَظِر خَطيبَته لأنَّه شَديد الأناقة ويَحمِل باقة من الزُهور الحَمراء. وماذا عَن هذا الرَجُل؟ يَبدو أنّه جاءَ لِيَستقبِل مُديره في العَمَل لأن مَلابِسه رَسميّة رَغم حَرارة الجَوّ كَما أنّه يحمل بعض الأوراق والمِلَفّات.

كان الزِحام شَديداً وكُلّما خَرَجَ أحَد الرُّكّاب جَرَى نَحوَه شَخص لِيَحتَضِنه. كانَت هناك قُبلات، ودُموع، وفَرَح، وأحضان. أطفال يَجرون ويَصيحون، ورِجال بِشَوارِب كَثيفة يُقَبِّلون أَيدي أُمَّهاتهم. كلّ هذه المَشاهِد المُؤَثِّرة مَرَّت أمام زهرة وكَأَنّها مَشاهِد من فيلم سينِمائيّ، فَمَرَّ الوَقت سَريعاً.

تَجَوَّلَتْ *she wandered*
قاعة الوُصول *arrivals hall*
إعلانات *advertisements*
عُطور *perfumes*
تَأجير السيّارات *car rental*
تُراقِب الناس *observing people*
تَتَخَيَّل *imagining*
رُبَّما *perhaps*
لِتَستَقبِلَ *to greet/receive*
خَطيبة *fiancée*
شَديد الأَناقة *very elegant*
باقة *bouquet*
يَبدو *it seems/appears*
رَسميّ *formal/official*
مِلَفّات *files*
زِحام *crowdedness*
كُلّما *whenever*
لِيَحتَضِنَهُ *to hug him*
قُبلات *kisses*
دُموع *tears*
أحضان *hugs*
شَوارِب كَثيفة *thick moustaches*
أيدي... *hands of...*
مَشاهِد مُؤَثِّرة *moving scenes*
مَرَّ الوَقت *the time passed*

After reading بعد القراءة

A Test your understanding.

1 How early did Zahra arrive at the airport?

2 What type of advertisements did she read in the airport while waiting?

3 Who did she imagine the woman was waiting to greet?

4 Who did she imagine the young man was waiting for? Why?

5 And the businessman, whom did she think he was waiting for? Why?

6 Was the airport crowded?

7 What were the children doing?

8 Did Zahra get bored waiting for Jamal? Why not?

B Complete these sentences about Zahra's time at the airport.

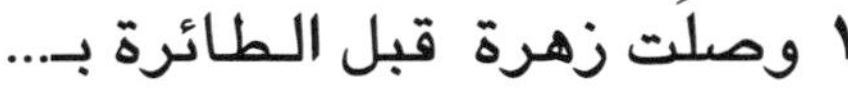

١ وصلَت زهرة قبل الطائرة بـ...

٢ في المطار قرأت زهرة...

٣ جلسَت تتخيّل قِصَص...

٤ كان الشاب يحمل...

٥ كان الرجل يلبس...

٦ كان الرجل يحمل...

٧ كان الجوّ...

٨ كان الأطفال يجرون و...

٩ كان الرجال يُقبّلون أيدي...

١٠ مرّ الوقت...

إلى المطار

Sounds of the City أصوات المدينة

كان هناك المَزيد من العَواطِف والأحضان حين وَصَلَت زهرة مع جمال إلى بيت خالته.

المَزيد من *more (increase of)*
عَواطِف *emotions*

قَضى الجَميع لَيلَتهُم يَضحَكون ويَتَحَدَّثون في مَواضيع مُختَلِفة حتّى نَسمات الفَجر الأولَى. بهيجة رَأَت في جمال وَسامة عدنان التي أسَرَت قَلب أختها بسمة مُنذُ حوالي ٢٥ عاماً. وجمال رَأَى في خالته بهيجة نُسخة من أمّه، ولكنّها نسخة أقَلّ بَريقاً بسبب المَرَض. وأمّا زهرة فإنّها رَكَّزَت على التَشابُه بين جمال وأخيها فادي، ذلك التشابه الذي يأتي من صِلة الدَم الواحد.

الجَميع *everyone*
يضحكون *laughing*
مَواضيع *subjects/topics*
نَسمات الفَجر *breezes of dawn*
وَسامة *handsomeness*
أَسَرَت *captivated*
نُسخة *copy*
أَقَلّ بَريقاً *less vibrant*
رَكَّزَت *[she] concentrated*
تَشابُه *likeness/similarity*
صِلة الدَم الواحِد *blood relation*

وبعد فَترة ذَهَبَ كلّ مِنهُم إلى حُجرَته لِيَنام قَليلاً، ولكن جمال وَجَدَ بعضَ الصُعوبة في النَوم رغم أنّه كان يَشعُر بالتَعَب بعد رِحلَته الطويلة الشّاقة. كان كلّ شيء حَولَه مختلفاً، السَرير والوِسادة، والصُوَر التي على الحائِط، والأصوات القادِمة من الشُبّاك. أصوات المدينة وهي تَبدَأ يَوماً جَديداً.

بَعدَ فَترة *after a while*
بَعضَ الصُعوبة *some difficulty*
تَعَب *tiredness*
شاقّ *hard/tiring*
وِسادة *pillow*

After reading بعد القراءة

A Test your understanding.

1 Jamal has arrived at...
a the hospital. b his aunt's house. c a hotel.

2 The family stayed up until dawn...
a working. b eating dinner. c laughing and talking.

3 Bahija noticed a strong resemblence between Jamal and...
a her brother. b his father. c his grandfather.

4 Jamal thought his aunt Bahija is a carbon copy of...
a his mother. b her daughter. c his grandmother.

5 Zahra concentrated on the resemblence between Jamal and...
a her brother. b her father. c her uncle.

6 When Jamal went to bed he...
a slept like a log. b took some photos. c was tired but couldn't sleep.

B Find the Arabic phrases in the reading passage with the following meanings.

1 talking about different subjects

2 to sleep a little

3 the first breezes of dawn

4 (as) it begins a new day

5 an exact likeness [copy] of his mother

6 he was feeling tired

7 about 25 years ago

8 captivated the heart of her sister

History Everywhere التاريخ في كُلّ مَكان

عَزيزي داني،

لَيتك كُنتَ معي أمس أثناءَ جَولتي في دمشق القديمة. أَخَذتُ أمس أكثر من سِتين صورة. التاريخ هنا موجود في كلّ مكان. يُمكِنك أن تَراه، وتَسمَعه، وتَتذَوَّقه، وتَشُمّه، وتَلمسه. كلّ هذه الأصوات والرَّوائِح والأشكال والألوان... كلّ البَضائِع والمَعروضات في الأسواق... واللافِتات فوق الدَّكاكين... الشَوارِع الضَيِّقة هنا لَم تَتَغَيَّر كثيراً منذ مِئات السِنين.

سوق الحميديّة مختلف تَماماً. مَثَلاً، عِندنا في كاليفورنيا لَو كان دُكّان يَبيع مَضارِب التنس، فإن جاره لَن يبيع مضارب التنس أيضاً. أمّا هنا فلو كان هناك دكّان يبيع مضارب التنس، فَسَتَجِد أن الشارِع كلّه يبيع مضارب التنس. أنا لا أعرِف كيف يعمل هذا النِظام الفَريد في التِّجارة، ولكنّه يعمل بِدون شَكّ. هذه الدكاكين موجودة وتعمل من مئات السنين. إنهُم يَعرِفون شيئاً هنا عن التجارة لا نَعرِفه نَحنُ في أمريكا.

مع تَحِياتي، جمال

* لا تَخَف يا داني، فأنا لم أنسَ طَلبك. طاولة الزهر في حَقيبَتي.

لَيتك كُنتَ... I wish you were...

جَولتي my tour

يُمكنِك أن... you can...

...تَتَذَوَّقه ...taste it

...تلَمِسه ...touch it

بَضائع goods/products

مَعروضات items on display

لافِتات فَوقَ الدكاكين signs above the shops

لَم تَتَغَيَّر haven't changed

لَو كان if there is

تَماماً completely

مَضارِب التَنِس tennis rackets

جارُه his neighbor

نِظام فَريد unique system

بِدون شَكّ without doubt

لا تَخَف don't worry/fear not

لَم أنسَ I didn't forget

طَلَبك your request

After reading
بعد القراءة

سوق الحَميديّة، دِمشَق

A Test your understanding.

1 Where was Jamal yesterday?
2 How many photos did he take?
3 Are the streets wide or narrow?
4 For how long does Jamal think the scene has remained unchanged?
5 What is the name of the market he visited?
6 Jamal writes that if a shop in California sells tennis rackets its neighbor will not do the same. How does he compare this to Damascus?

B Find the plurals of the words below in Jamal's letter.

Meaning	Singular	Plural
sound	صَوت	
shape	شَكل	
color	لَون	
market	سوق	
(shop) sign	لافِتة	
shop/store	دُكّان	
racket	مِضرَب	
year	سَنة	

10 Two Rooms in Beirut غُرفتان في بيروت

بعد جُهد، حَجَزَت زهرة غُرفتَين في فُندُق ثلاث نُجوم في بَيروت. غُرفة مُزدَوِجة لجمال وفادي، وغرفة لِشَخص واحِد لها. إنَّ العُثور على غرفة في فندق صعب في هذا الوَقت من السَنة لأن هناك عائِلات كَثيرة من دُوَل الخَليج تَقضي عُطلة الصَّيف في لُبنان.

بعد جُهد *after some effort*
ثَلاث نُجوم *3-star*
غُرفة مُزدَوِجة *double room*
العُثور على *finding/obtaining*
عائلات *families*
دُوَل الخَليج *the Gulf states*
عُطلة الصَّيف *summer vacation*

قَرَّرَت زهرة أن سيّارة أُجرة «سرفيس» هي أَفضَل وَسيلة لِلسفر إلى بيروت مع جمال وفادي لِقَضاء يَومَين. إن المَسافة بين دمشق وبيروت لَيسَت بَعيدة، ولكن لا يمكن لأَحَد أن يَعرِف كم سَتَستَغرِق الرحلة بالسيّارة. فهناك الزِحام على الطَريق بين دمشق وبيروت، وأيضاً الزحام عند عُبور الحُدود، ثُمَّ الزحام في بيروت نَفسها.

قَرَّرَت *[she] decided*
سَيّارة أُجرة *taxicab*
وَسيلة *means/method*
لِقَضاء *(in order) to spend*
مَسافة *distance*
لا يُمكِن لأَحَد *no one could*
سَتَستَغرِق *would last*
عُبور الحُدود *crossing the border*

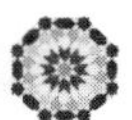

After reading بعد القراءة

A Test your understanding.

1 What type of rooms did Zahra reserve in Beirut?

2 Why was it difficult to find rooms?

3 How did they travel from Damascus to Beirut?

4 What do people in the region call this method of transportation?

5 How long was their stay in Beirut?

6 Why don't they know how long the journey will take?

B Decide if these Arabic sentences about the text are true or false.

١ ذهب جمال إلى بيروت مع ابن وابنة خالته.

٢ حجزَت زهرة غُرفتين مُزدوِجتين في الفندق.

٣ هناك عائلات كثيرة في بيروت في شهور الصيف.

٤ يذهب اللبنانيّون إلى دُوَل الخليج لِعُطلة الصيف.

٥ سافر جمال وفادي وزهرة إلى بيروت بالقطار.

٦ إنَّ مدينة دمشق ليسَت بعيدة عن بيروت.

٧ هناك زحام على الطريق بين المدينتين.

٨ ليس هناك زحام في بيروت نَفسها.

Many Accents لَهجات كثيرة

سَمِعَ جمال لَهجات كثيرة في بيروت. جمال لا يعرف الفَرق في اللَهجة بين الناس، فهو يَرى أنّهُم جميعاً يتحدّثون اللُّغة العربيّة. ولكن زهرة تعرف الفرق. فهي تَقول لجمال مثلاً، «هل سَمِعتَ هذا الرَجُل وهو يتحدّث؟ إنّه بَيروتيّ أَصليّ»، أو «هذه السيّدة فِلَسطينيّة بدون شكّ»، أو «هؤُلاءِ الشَّباب من جَنوب لبنان، أَكيد!»، وهكَذا.

فادي أيضاً يعرف اللهجات، ويَقول لجمال، «هذا الصَّبي عِراقيّ.»، أو «هذه الفَتاة من الريف.»، وسَألَ فادي جمال مَرّة، «هل سمعتَ هذا الشابّ وهو يتحدّث؟ هذه طَريقة سُكّان الجَبَل في الكَلام.»

ولكن جمال اِبتَسَمَ وقال، «يا عزيزي فادي، كَم أَنتَ ماهِر! أنت تَسمَع ما لا أَسمَعه أنا.»

لَهجات accents
فَرق difference
أَصليّ native/original
هؤلاء الشَّباب these young people
وَهكَذا and so on
صَبيّ boy
فَتاة girl/young woman
الريف the countryside
طَريقة way/style
سُكَّان inhabitants
اِبتَسَمَ smiled
ماهِر clever

After reading بعد القراءة

A Test your understanding.

1 Zahra pointed out three examples of Arabic accents. Where did she say the accents originated?
2 Fadi also pointed out people with different accents. Where were they from?
3 Could Jamal hear these differences? What phrases in the text tell you this?

B Match the Arabic expressions from the reading passage to the English equivalents.

a native Beiruti	١ سكّان الجبل
b once/one time	٢ من جنوب لبنان
c when/as he talks	٣ كم أنت ماهر
d mountain dwellers	٤ بدون شكّ
e how clever you are	٥ وهو يتحدّث
f without doubt	٦ طريقة في الكلام
g style of talking	٧ بيروتيّ أصليّ
h from the south of Lebanon	٨ مرّة

12 The Secret of Happiness سِرّ السَعادة

وبعد يومَين في بيروت، قال جمال لِزهرة وفادي وهم في طَريق العَودة، «أعجَبَتني بيروت كثيراً. إنّها مدينة مَليئة بالحَياة. مثلاً، رَأيتُ الفَتَيات يَمشينَ في الطريق معاً، مِنهُنَّ مَن تَرتَدي الحِجاب التَقليديّ ومنهنّ مَن ترتدي الجينز الأمريكيّ. رأيتُ مَطاعِم الوَجَبات السَّريعة جَنباً إلى جَنب مع مطاعم المَأكولات اللُبنانيّة التقليديّة. الناس هناك يَبدون سُعَداء بِهذا التَنَوُّع.»

قال فادي، «ولِمَ لا؟ بَلَدهُم صغير في الحَجم، ولكن فيه البَحر والجَبَل والشَمس الساطِعة والسَماء الزَّرقاء. فيه الفاكِهة الطَيِّبة والمأكولات اللَذيذة!»

قالَت زهرة، «ولكن أَهَمّ شيء هو أن اللبنانيّين دائِماً يُؤَدّون عَمَلهُم بِأَحسَن طريقة. الشابّ الذي كان يُجَهِّز السَّندَوِتشات في مطعم الشاوَرمة يُريد أن تَكون سندوتشاته هي أطيَب سندوتشات في المدينة! وفي رَأيي هذا هو سِرّ نَجاحهم. والنجاح يَأتي بالسَّعادة.»

- طَريق العَودة *the way back*
- أعجَبَتني *I liked (it pleased me)*
- مَليء بالحَياة *full of life*
- فَتَيات *young girls*
- مِنهُنَّ *amongst them*
- تَرتَدي *wearing*
- تَقليديّ *traditional*
- الوَجَبات السَريعة *fast food*
- جَنباً إلى جَنب *side by side*
- يَبدون *[they] appear/seem*
- سُعَداء *happy* (plural)
- التَّنَوُّع *variety/variation*
- لِمَ؟ *why?*
- في الحَجم *in size*
- ساطِع *bright/shining*
- الفاكِهة *fruit*
- يؤَدّون عَمَلَهُم *perform their work*
- كان يُجَهِّز *was preparing*
- الشاوَرمة *spit-roast*
- أطيَب *the tastiest*
- في رَأيي *in my opinion*
- النَّجاح *success*
- السَّعادة *happiness*

After reading بعد القراءة

A Test your understanding.

1 Did Jamal like Beirut?

2 What two examples does he give of the traditional and modern sitting happily side by side?

3 Fadi gives a number of reasons why the Lebanese have cause to be happy. Can you find three of these reasons?

4 What does Zahra think about the work ethic of the Lebanese?

5 What specific job does Zahra give as an example of this work ethic?

B Make changes to phrases in the text to express the following in Arabic.

1 after two weeks in Beirut
2 I liked Damascus a lot
3 a city full of variety
4 traditional American dishes
5 their country is large in size
6 the delicious fruit
7 the best thing
8 the most important city
9 the girl who was preparing the sandwiches
10 in the fish restaurant
11 in our opinion
12 the people are happy with this success

الناس سُعَداء بهذا التَّنَوُّع

Review 2

المراجعة ٢

وَصَلَت زهرة إلى المطار قبل موعد الطائرة بحوالي ساعة لِتَستَقبِل جمال وتَعود به إلى بيت خالته. هناك، قَضَى الجميع لَيلَتهُم يَضحِكون ويتحدّثون في مواضيع مختلفة.

وفي الصباح زار جمال سوق دمشق القديمة. وبعد عَودَته إلى البيت كَتَبَ رِسالة إلى صديقه داني وَصَفَ فيها الدكاكين ونِظامها الفَريد في التِّجارة. نظام لم يتغيَّر منذ مئات السنين.

ذهب جمال مع زهرة وفادي لِقَضاء يومَين في بيروت. وهناك سمع لَهجات كثيرة من الناس الذين يتحدّثون اللغة العربية. زهرة وفادي يَعرِفان الفَرق بين هذه اللهجات. وفي طريق العودة، قال جمال لزهرة وفادي إن بيروت أَعجَبَته كثيراً لأنّها مدينة مَليئة بالحياة.

قالَت زهرة لجمال إن أهمّ شيء هو أن اللبنانيّين دائماً يُؤَدّون عملهم بأحسن طريقة. وفي رَأيها هذا هو سِرّ نَجاحهم. والنجاح يأتي بالسَّعادة.

Vocabulary review مُراجَعة المُفرَدات

1 d	i	s	h	e	2 s	

Across
1 مَأكولات (5)
6 فَريد (6)
7 طائِرة (8)
8 سِنين (5)
10 سوق (6)
12 مَضارِب التَّنِس (6,7)
13 دِمشَق (8)
14 يَضحكون (4,5)
16 يَعرِف (2,5)
17 سُكّان (11)

Down
2 نَجاح (7)
3 سِرّ (6)
4 بَيروت (6)
5 سَعادة (9)
9 رَأي (7)
11 تَقليديّ (11)
15 لَهجة (6)

Jamal's Blog: Day 1 مُدَوَّنة جمال: يوم ١

رحلة جمال في الشرق الأوسط

أنا أقضي وقتاً مُمتِعاً في الأردُنّ رغم أنّني أمشي كثيراً. أَغلَب البُيوت في عمّان لَونها أبيَض. تُذَكِّرني هذه البيوت البَيضاء بِصُوَر جُزُر اليونان. التِلال في عمّان مَوجودة في كلّ مكان، والبيوت مَبنِية على هذه التلال. أنا أَشعُر أن عمّان مختلفة عن دمشق، ولكن في نَفس الوقت أشعر أنها تَتَشابَه معها. هل تَفهَمون قَصدي؟ أنا أشعر أن عمّان قَد تَكون اِبنة عَمّ دمشق، أو اِبنة خالتها، ولكن لَيسَت أختها.

اليوم تَجَوَّلتُ كثيراً حول المدينة، وبعد أن تَعِبتُ من المَشي، جَلَستُ في مَقهَى تَقليديّ لأشرب الشاي في كوب صغير مثل أهل البَلَد. السُكّر كثير، ولكن لا مانِع. إن أَرَدتَ أن تَشرَب الشاي أو القَهوة هنا، فإن الاِختِيارات المُتاحة لَكَ كثيرة مثل المَقاهي الأمريكيّة أو الأُوروبيّة، ولكنّي أُفَضِّل الجُلوس في مقهى تقليديّ لأنّني أُريد أن أشعر أنّني في الشرق الأوسط.

مُمتِع *enjoyable*

أَغلَب... *most of...*

تُذَكِّرني بِـ *[they] remind me of*

تِلال *hills*

مَبنِية *built*

تَتَشابَه مَعها *resemble each other*

قَد يَكون *might be/could be*

تَعِبتُ من المَشي *I tired of walking*

لا مانِع *I don't mind*

المُتاحة لك *available to you*

المَقاهي *the cafés*

After reading بعد القراءة

A Test your understanding.

1 Jamal is writing his blog from Amman in...
  a Jordan. b Syria. c Egypt.

2 Most of the houses in Amman are...
  a multicolored. b white. c large.

3 Jamal is reminded of houses he has seen in pictures of...
  a the Greek Islands. b Illinois.
  c the Arabian peninsula.

4 Jamal describes the relationship between Amman and Damascus as similar to that between...
  a sisters. b mother and daughter. c cousins.

5 Jamal tells us he has spent a lot of his time in Amman...
  a buying souvenirs. b hill climbing. c walking the streets.

6 Jamal prefers to drink coffee in...
  a traditional cafés. b American cafés. c European cafés.

7 Traditional Arabic tea is served...
  a in small glasses with a lot of sugar. b in small glasses with no sugar.
  c in small cups with milk.

أشرب الشاي مثل أهل البَلَد

Jamal's Blog: Day 2 مُدَوَّنة جمال: يوم ٢

رحلة جمال في الشرق الأوسط

أمس، في طريقي إلى «بَترا» بالقِطار جلستُ بِجانِب الشبّاك لأَستَمتِع بالمَناظِر الصَّحراوِيّة الجَميلة. الجَوّ هنا بِلا تَلَوُّث والرُّؤية واضِحة لِمَسافات بَعيدة. لا تُوجد رُطوبة في الجوّ هنا مثل الرطوبة الموجودة في بيروت. الجوّ حارّ، ولكنّه جافّ.

اليوم اِستَيقظتُ الساعة الخامسة والنصف صباحاً لأَكسِب ساعتَين أو ثلاث من المشي في بَترا قبل أن تَرتَفِع دَرَجة الحَرارة. يمكن أن تَقرَأ عن بترا، أو عن العَصر الرومانيّ لِتَحصُل على بعض المَعلومات التاريخيّة. ويمكنك أيضاً أن ترى الكُهوف والمَقابِر في الصُّوَر أو على الاِنتَرنت. ولكنّني اليوم مشَيتُ في ذلَك المَمَرّ الضيّق بين جُدران الجبل الشاهِقة حتّى وصلتُ إلى الآثار المَنحوتة في الصُخور الوَرديّة. وهنا، شعرتُ أنّني إنسان صغير الحَجم يَقِف أمام إنجاز عِملاق. كُنتُ في وَسَط عالَم آخَر لا تَصِل إلَيه الصور أو الانترنت.

بَترا Petra (more formally البَتراء)
لأستَمتِع to enjoy
صَحراويّ desert (adj.)
بِلا تَلَوُّث without pollution
رُؤية visibility
رُطوبة humidity
جافّ dry
اِستَيقَظتُ I woke up
لأكسِب to gain
تَرتَفِع rises
العَصر الرومانيّ Roman era
مَعلومات information
كُهوف caves
مَقابِر tombs
مَمَرّ corridor
شاهِق towering
آثار ruins
مَنحوت carved
إنجاز achievement
عِملاق giant

After reading بعد القراءة

A Test your understanding.

1 How does Jamal travel through the desert?
2 Jamal compares the dryness of the desert to the humidity of which town?
3 What time did he wake up today? Why?
4 What does Jamal say you can read about or see on the Internet?
5 How does he feel when he finally reaches Petra?

B Identify the adjectives in the blog and make sure you know what they mean. Then see if you can use them to put the following into Arabic.

(Remember to use a *feminine singular* adjective to describe non-human plurals.)

1 a pink shirt
2 a historic town
3 narrow streets
4 a desert road
5 beautiful caves
6 towering mountains
7 clear information
8 distant hills
9 a small-sized house
10 Roman ruins

المَمَرّ الضيّق بين جُدران الجبل الشاهِقة

Jamal's Blog: Day 3 مُدَوَّنة جمال: يوم ٣

رحلة جمال في الشرق الأوسط

من بترا إلى خَليج العَقَبة مُنحدَر واحد طويل يَتَّجِه جَنوباً نَحوَ ساحِل البحر الأحمَر. الطريق يَهبُط أكثر من ألف متر، ويَمُرّ على مَناجِم الفوسفات المشهورة وعلى مِنطَقة «وادي رُم». الوادي يَبدو مثل سَطح القَمر بسبب أشكال الصخور ولون الرمال. أنا قَرَأتُ في الدَليل السّياحيّ أن المُخرِجين يُحِبّون هذا الوادي كَمَوقع لِتصوير الأفلام السِّينِمائيّة. كنتُ أَوَدّ أن أزور وادي رم ولكن لِلأَسف وَقتي مَحدود.

حين وصلتُ إلى العقبة وَقَفتُ على الشاطئ ونَظَرتُ حولي. إن العقبة مثل مُفتَرَق الطُّرُق. كلّ اِتِّجاه هنا سَيَأخُذك إلى بلد مختلف. غداً سَيَكون يوماً مُهِمّاً في حَياتي لأنّني سَأَعبر من آسيا إلى إفريقيا. عندي حَجز على العَبّارة المُتَّجِهة إلى ميناء نويبَع في سيناء.

يوم جديد ومُغامَرة جديدة في رحلة رائِعة.

مُنحَدَر incline/slope
يَتَّجِه نَحو heading toward
يَهبُط falls/goes down
مَناجِم mines
سَطح surface
دَليل سِياحيّ tourist guide
مُخرِجون/ين [movie] directors
كُنتُ أوَدّ I would have liked
وَقَفتُ I stood
مُفتَرَق الطُرُق crossroads
اِتِّجاه direction
سَأعبُر I will cross
عَبّارة ferry
مُغامَرة adventure
رائِع fantastic/marvelous

After reading بعد القراءة

A Test your understanding.

1 The road from Petra to the Gulf of Aqaba is one long incline...
a west. b south. c north.

2 The Gulf of Aqaba is part of...
a the Mediterranean. b the Suez Canal. c the Red Sea.

3 Jamal passes mines producing...
a fossil fuel. b phosphate. c silver.

4 Wadi Rum is popular as a movie location because...
a the desert has unusual features. b it looks like Hollywood.
c it is in the tourist guides.

5 Jamal descibes Aqaba as being like...
a a busy traffic junction. b a different country.
c a crossing point between continents.

6 The next day Jamal is taking the ferry heading to...
a Asia. b Sinai. c Sana'a.

وادي رُم يَبدو مثل سَطح القمر

16 Jamal's Blog: Day 4 مُدَوَّنة جمال: يوم ٤

رحلة جمال في الشرق الأوسط

أَخَذتُ العبّارة وعَبَرتُ من آسيا إلى إفريقيا. في الحَقيقة، لم أرَ فرقاً شاسِعاً بين ميناء العقبة الأُردُنّيّ، وميناء نوَيبَع المِصريّ. نفس الزحام والصِّياح والصِّراع لِتَكسَب سَنتيمرات من سيّارة بِجانِبك. الحافِلات مَليئة بالمُسافِرين، والسيّارات تَكاد تَلمس الأَسفَلت تَحت أحمالها: حَقائِب سفر، صَناديق، أكياس بلاستِك كبيرة مَلفوفة بِخُيوط سَميكة، وعُلَب كَرتون كبيرة. فهذا يَحمِل مِروَحة يابانيّة، وهذا اِشتَرَى تليفزيون صينيّ، وآخر معه ثَلاجة مُتَوَسِّطة الحَجم من كوريا.

شاسِع *wide/huge*
نَفس الـ... *the same...*
صِراع *struggle*
مُسافِرون/ين *passengers*
تَكاد تَلمس *nearly touching*
مَلفوف *wrapped*
خُيوط سَميكة *thick cords*
مِروَحة *fan*

العبّارة كانَت مَليئة بالمُدَرِّسين والمُهَندِسين والعُمّال والمُوَظِّفين المِصريّين. كانوا كلّهم في طريقهم من دُوَل الخليج إلى مصر لِقضاء عطلة الصيف مع أَهلهم. جاءَ بعضهم من الكوَيت، وبعضهم من الإمارات، أو قَطَر أو البَحرَين، ولكن جاءَ أغلَبهُم من السُعوديّة. لا بُدّ أن هذه الرِّحلات كانَت شاقّة، وبِرغم شِدّة الحَرارة والزحام، كانوا يضحكون ويُغَنّون ويَبدون سُعَداء لأنّهم اِقتَرَبوا من بلدهم.

عُمّال *workers*
مُوَظَّفون/ين *employees*
بَعضهُم *some of them*
أغلَبهُم *most of them*
شِدّة *intensity/strength*
يُغَنّون *[they were] singing*
اِقترَبوا *they were approaching*

After reading بعد القراءة

A Test your understanding.

1 What is Jamal's immediate impression of Nuweiba? What gave him this impression?
2 What four types of loads does Jamal mention seeing on top of the cars on the ferry?
3 What three specific household appliances does Jamal mention?
4 Jamal mentions five Gulf countries that the Egyptian passengers are returning from. What are they?
5 Which country does he say most of them are returning from?

B Match the Arabic expressions from the reading passage to the English equivalents.

a a huge difference	١ حقائب سفر
b extreme heat	٢ في طريقهم من
c beneath their loads	٣ فرق شاسع
d cardboard boxes	٤ لم أرَ
e I didn't see	٥ في الحقيقة
f travel cases	٦ عُلَب كرتون
g on their way from	٧ تحت أحمالها
h actually/in truth	٨ شدة الحرارة

Review 3

المراجعة ٣

تَجَوَّلَ جمال وَحده في عمّان. وكان يمشي كثيراً لِيرى المدينة. وفي طريقه إلى البتراء بالقطار جَلَسَ بجانب الشبّاك لِيَستَمتِعِ بالمناظر الصحراويّة الجميلة. ومن البتراء اِتَّجَهَ جنوباً إلى خليج العَقَبة لِيَعبر من آسيا إلى إِفريقيا في مُغامرة جديدة.

العبّارة التي أخذها جمال من آسيا إلى سيناء في إفريقيا كانت مليئة بالسيّارات والحافلات والمسافرين. كانوا كلّهم مصريين في طريقهم من دول الخليج إلى مصر لقضاء العطلة الصيفيّة مع أهلهم. جاء بعضهم من الكويت، وبعضهم من الإمارات، أو قطر أو البحرين، ولكن جاء أغلبهم من السعوديّة.

من هؤلاء المسافرين من كان يَحمِل مِروَحة يابانيّة، وآخر معه تليفزيون صينيّ، وهذا معه ثَلاجة مُتَوَسِّطة الحَجم من كوريا. لا بُدّ أن هذه الرِّحلات كانَت شاقّة عليهم، بسبب شِدّة الحَرارة والزحام.

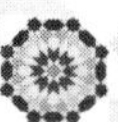

Vocabulary review مُراجَعة المُفرَدات

1 r
u
i
n
s

ACROSS

2 رُطوبة (8)

3 قَطَر (5)

6 تِلال (5)

9 حَرارة (4)

10 عُمّال (7)

12 مُغامَرة (9)

13 عَبّارة (5)

16 اِتّجاه (9)

17 تَجَوَّل (2,8)

18 قِطار (5)

19 عُطلة الصَّيف (6,8)

DOWN

1 آثار (5)

4 القَمر (3,4)

5 البَتراء (5)

7 اِستَيقَظتُ (1,4,2)

8 صَحراء (6)

11 خَليج العَقَبة (4,2,5)

14 مَناظِر (5)

15 كُهوف (5)

17 Jamal's Blog: Day 5 مُدَوَّنة جمال: يوم ٥

رحلة جمال في الشرق الأوسط

من نويبع اتَّجَهتُ إلى دَير سانت كاثرين. رأيتُ بعض الجِمال تَسير وَحدها في الصَحراء. رُبَّما كانت جمالاً بَرّيّة أو ربّما كانت مَملوكة لِبَدَويّ تَرَكَها تَرعَى. لا بُدّ أنّها تعرف طريق العودة إلى صاحِبها. لاحَظتُ أن مَلابِس البَدو بيضاء وواسِعة لِتُناسِب الطَّقس الحارّ، وأمّا السيِّدات فمَلابِسهُنَّ واسعة أيضاً، ولكنّها سَوداء. لا أعرف لِماذا، فاللّون الأسود يَجتَذِب الحرارة. رُبَّما هو لُغز من ألغاز الصحراء!

الفرق شاسِع بين ضَوضاء الميناء وسُكون الدَّير. في المساء اِتَّفَقتُ مع شابَّين من السويد، وآخر من الأرجنتين، وفَتاتَين من اِسكتلندا على أن نَستَيقِظ معاً حوالي الساعة الثانية بعد مُنتَصَف اللّيل لِنَتَسَلَّق جَبَل موسى معاً لِنَرى شُروق الشَّمس من فوق القِمّة.

وحين بَدَأنا في التَسَلُّق، كان هناك غَيرنا كثيرون لدَيهم نَفس المَشروع! شَباب وشابّات من حول العالم كلّهم يُريدون نَفس الشيء.

- دَير *monastery*
- تَسير *walking (along)*
- بَرّيّ *wild*
- تَرَكَها تَرعَى *left them to graze*
- لاحَظتُ *I noticed*
- لِتُناسِب *to be suitable for*
- يَجتَذِب *attracts*
- لُغز من ألغاز *one of the mysteries*
- ضَوضاء *noise/din*
- اِتَّفَقتُ *I agreed*
- مُنتَصَف اللّيل *midnight*
- لِنَتَسَلَّق *[in order] to climb*
- قِمّة *summit*
- حين بَدَأنا *when we began*
- مَشروع *project/scheme*

After reading بعد القراءة

A Test your understanding.

1 Where is Jamal writing this blog from?
2 What did he see roaming in the desert?
3 What color is the men's clothing among the Bedouin?
4 What about the women's clothing?
5 Who did he link up with to climb Mount Moses?
6 What time did they set out for the climb?
7 What were they hoping to witness from the summit?
8 Who else was on the mountain?

B Decide if these Arabic sentences about the text are true or false.

١ ملابس البدو واسعة.

٢ ملابس الرجال سوداء.

٣ هناك جِمال في الصحراء.

٤ ليس هناك فرق بين العقبة والدير.

٥ قابل جمال شابَّين من اسكتلندا.

٦ قابل شابّاً من الأرجنتين.

٧ استيقظ جمال الساعة الثانية بعد الظهر.

٨ كان هناك شَباب كثيرون يَتَسَلَّقون جبل موسى.

دَير سانت كاثرين

A Card from Egypt بَطاقة من مصر

عزيزتي زهرة وعزيزي فادي،

قَضيتُ نصف يوم في شَرَم الشّيخ، واِشتَرَيتُ من هناك بعض الهَدايا والتِّذكارات. شربتُ عَصيراً مصريّاً لذيذاً وهو خَليط من فواكِه مَوسِميّة مَمزوجة في الخَلاط مع السكّر والثّلج. كان فيه مانجو وشَمّام ومَوز وفَراولة. كم كان رائعاً!

غداً سَآخذ طائرة مصر للطَيران إلى القاهِرة في الصباح الباكِر وسأقضي هناك يوماً واحداً أزور فيه الأهرام. سأعود إلى دمشق في المساء.

رحلتي اِقتَرَبَت من نِهايَتها للأسف. كنتُ أودّ أن أَبقَى هنا شهرَين أو ثلاثة.

مع حُبّي،

جمال

هَدايا *presents/gifts*

تِذكارات *souvenirs*

خَليط *mixture*

مَوسِميّ *seasonal*

مَمزوج *mixed/blended*

خَلاّط *blender*

ثَلج *ice*

شَمّام *melon/cantaloupe*

فَراولة *strawberry*

مِصر للطَيران *Egypt Air*

الصَّباح الباكِر *the early morning*

الأهرام *the Pyramids*

نِهايَتها *its end/its completion*

أن أبقَى *to stay/remain (that I stay)*

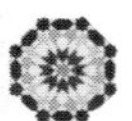

After reading بعد القراءة

A Test your understanding. Answer the questions in Arabic.

١ البطاقة من أيّة مدينة في مصر؟

٢ لِمَن كتب جمال البطاقة؟

٣ هل قضى جمال أسبوعاً هناك؟

٤ ماذا شرب؟

٥ متى سيأخذ الطائرة إلى القاهرة؟

٦ ماذا يُريد أن يزور هناك؟

٧ إلى أين سيذهب بعد القاهرة؟

٨ لماذا لا يبقى جمال في مصر لفترة أطول؟

B Put the following sentences into Arabic, using the text as a model.

1 I drank Syrian juice.
2 It is a mixture of summer fruits.
3 Tomorrow I will take the train to Cairo.
4 I spent two days in Sharm El-Sheikh.
5 I will return to Cairo in the morning.
6 I will spend half a day there in which I will visit the Pyramids.
7 My visit is nearing its completion, unfortunately.
8 I would have liked to buy some gifts.

19 On the Plane في الطائرة

الرحلة من شرم الشيخ إلى مَطار القاهرة كانت حوالي ساعة. الطائِرة كانت مَليئة بالسُّوّاح. كان هناك سائِح ضَخم الجُثّة في حوالي الخَمسين من العُمر، يَجلِس بجانب جمال. هذا الرجل كان يَملأ مِقعَده ويَفيض قَليلاً لِيَأخُذ جُزءاً من مِقعَد جمال على يَساره والمقعد الآخَر على يَمينه أيضاً. يَبدو أنّه نَسِيَ ونام في الشَّمس على الشاطِئ لأن صُلعَته كانَت حَمراء مُتَوَهِّجة كَالفَحم في مطعم المَشوِيات وأَنفه أحمَر وبِلا جِلد مِثل ثَمرة الطَماطِم الناضِجة بَعدَ تَقشيرها. شَفَته العُليا كانت مُغَطّاة تَماماً بالكريم الخاصّ بِعِلاج الحُروق.

لَم يَكُن الرجل مُرتاحاً على مقعد الدَّرَجة السِّياحيّة. كان كثير الحَرَكة بَحثاً عَن الوَضع الأمثَل. ومع كلّ حركة كان جمال يَتَلَقّى كوعاً في ضُلوعه، أو كَتِفاً في رَقَبَته، أو ذِراعاً في صَدره.

- سائِح/سُوّاح *tourist/tourists*
- ضَخم الجثّة *heavily built*
- يَفيض *spilling over*
- جُزء من *a part of*
- نَسِيَ *he forgot*
- صُلعته *his bald patch*
- مُتَوَهَّجة *glowing*
- فَحم *charcoal/coal*
- المَشويات *grilled food*
- جِلد *skin*
- ناضِجة *ripe*
- تَقشير *peeling*
- شَفته العُليا *his upper lip*
- مُغَطّاة *covered*
- عِلاج الحُروق *treating [sun]burn*
- مُرتاح *comfortable/at ease*
- الدَّرَجة السياحية *tourist class*
- بَحثا عَن *searching for*
- الوَضع الأمثَل *the ideal position*
- يَتلَقّى *receiving*

After reading بعد القراءة

A Test your understanding.

1 Jamal travelled from Sharm el-Skeikh to Cairo by...

a plane. b bus. c ferry.

2 He sat next to...

a an Egyptian. b a young tourist. c a middle-aged tourist.

3 The tourist was...

a young but heavily built. b bald and heavily built. c bald and thin.

4 The text speculates that Jamal's neighbor was sunburned because...

a he has no hair. b he fell asleep in the sun.

c he forgot his sun cream.

5 The man had sunburn cream on...

a his nose. b his bald patch. c his upper lip.

6 Jamal was uncomfortable because the tourist kept...

a poking him when he moved. b adjusting Jamal's seat.

c adjusting his own seat.

B The following parts of the body are mentioned in the text. Can you find the Arabic words?

1 nose
2 chest
3 neck
4 arm
5 shoulder
6 ribs
7 lip
8 elbow

صلعته كانت حمراء متوهّجة

20 The Pyramids الأهرام

في مطار القاهرة وجد جمال سائِق تاكسي يبدو طيِّب القَلب. عُمره حَوالي ستّين عاماً وكان يَرتَدي قُبَّعة قُطنيّة بَيضاء ونظّارة شمس رَخيصة. بعد حِوار قَصير اِتَّفق السائِق مع جمال على أن يأخذه في جَولة طَوال اليوم ثمّ يعود به إلى المطار في العاشِرة مَساءً ليأخذ الطائرة المُتَّجِهة إلى دمشق. جَلَس جمال بجانب السائق على المِقعَد الأماميّ وبِسُرعة وسُهولة أَصبَحا مِثل صَديقَين، وانطَلَقا في شَوارِع القاهرة باِتِّجاه الأهرام.

قضى جمال في مِنطَقة الأهرام حوالي ساعة. رَكِبَ جَمَلاً اسمه منصور في جولة قَصيرة وأَخَذ صُوَراً كثيرة للأهرام وأبو الهول. صاحِب الجمل طَلَبَ ثلاثين دولاراً لنفسه، وعشرين دولاراً أخرى للجمل لأن منصور لا يحبّ أن يُصَوِّره أحد. بعد حِوار ضاحِك أَعطاه جمال خَمسة دولارات لَهُ ودولاراً لِمنصور. ووَعَدَه أن يَعود في العام القادِم ويُحضِر له قبّعة من تكساس كَهَدِية له، وبَعض التُّفّاح الأمريكيّ الفاخِر كَهَدِية لِمنصور.

سائِق *driver*
طيِّب القَلب *kindhearted*
قُبَّعة *hat*
حِوار *dialogue/discussion*
جَولة *tour*
بِسُرعة وسُهولة *quickly and easily*
اِنطَلَقا *[they both] set off*
مِنطَقة *area/district*
أبو الهول *the Sphinx*
صاحِب *owner*
يُصَوِّره *to photograph him*
ضاحِك *light-hearted/amusing*
وَعَدَه *he promised him*
كَهَدِية *as a gift*
فاخِر *first-class/excellent*

After reading بعد القراءة

A Test your understanding. Answer the questions in Arabic.

١ كيف ذهب جمال من المطار إلى الأهرام؟

٢ كم عمر السائق تقريباً؟

٣ ماذا كان يلبس السائق؟

٤ هل جلس جمال وراء السائق؟

٥ ماذا فعل جمال في منطقة الأهرام؟

٦ ما هو اسم الجمل؟

٧ كم طلب صاحب الجمل لنفسه؟ وكم طلب لمنصور؟

٨ وكم أعطاه جمال بعد الحوار؟

٩ بماذا وعد جمال صاحب الجمل كهدية له؟

١٠ وبماذا وعده كهدية لمنصور؟

منصور لا يحبّ أن يُصَوِّره أحَد

The Night of Travel ليلة السفر

جلسَت الأسرة في غُرفة الجُلوس بعد العَشاء. كانوا يَشعُرون أن شيئاً جميلاً يَقتَرِب من نِهايَته. اِحتَضَنَت بهيجة ابن أختها وقالَت، «أنا لا أُصدِّق أن العُطلة اِنتَهَت وأنّك سَتعود إلى أمريكا غداً. هل اِستَمتَعتَ بِرحلَتك؟».

رَدَّ جمال، «اِستَمتَعتُ بِكلّ دَقيقة يا خالتي. لم أشعر أنّني غَريب، ولم أشعر بِالوَحدة أبَداً.» قالَت زهرة، «ما هو أكثر شيء أَعجَبك؟» وقال فادي، «وما هو أكثر شيء أَزعَجك!»

قال جمال، «في الحقيقة أَزعَجني شيء واحِد فَقَط، ولكن أَعجَبَتني أشياء كثيرة جدّاً. ما أَزعَجني هو طَريقة قِيادة السيّارات. السائِقون يَقودون سيّاراتهم بِسُرعة كَأنّ الحَياة تَنتَهي غداً، ويَستَخدِمون الأبواق كثيراً. أما الأشياء التي أَعجَبَتني فهي المَأكولات والمِعمار القديم والآثار والطَّقس. أَعجَبَني الشُعور بِالتاريخ في كلّ مكان. أَحبَبتُ الناس وكَرَمهم رغم صُعوبات الحَياة، وكيف يضحكون فَيَحِلّون المشاكل فيما بَينَهُم.»

غُرفة الجُلوس *sitting room*
اِحتَضَنَت *[she] hugged*
أنا لا أُصدِّق *I don't believe*
اِنتَهَت *has finished*
هل اِستَمتَعتَ؟ *did you enjoy?*
دَقيقة *minute*
غَريب *a stranger*
وَحدة *loneliness*
أَعجَبَك *pleased you*
أَزعَجك *bothered you*
قِيادة السيّارات *driving*
يَقودون *[they] drive*
أبواق *[car] horns*
كَرَمهم *their generosity*
صُعوبات *difficulties*
يَحِلّون *[they] solve*
فيما بَينَهُم *among themselves*

After reading بعد القراءة

A Test your understanding.

1 Who is Jamal sitting with?
2 When is he flying back to America?
3 Did he feel lonely while he was on vacation?
4 What was the one thing that bothered him and why?
5 Name at least four things Jamal mentions that he liked about his trip.
6 What two characteristics does Jamal like about the people in the region?

أحبَبتُ الناس وكيف يضحكون

B What is the meaning of these phrases that appear in the text?

١ بعد العشاء	٦ لم أشعر بالوحدة
٢ كلّ دقيقة	٧ أكثر شيء أعجبك
٣ أشياء كثيرة	٨ يستخدمون الأبواق كثيراً
٤ في الحقيقة	٩ رغم صعوبات الحياة
٥ المعمار القديم	١٠ كأنّ الحياة تنتهي غداً

22 Packing the Case إعداد الحقيبة

بدَأَ جمال في إعداد حَقيبَته لِلسفر، وقال، «الأسعار هنا أَرخَص من أمريكا. أنا معي هَدايا كثيرة لأصدِقائي هناك.» سَأَلَته زهرة عنَ القُرط الفِضّيّ الجميل الموجود في الحقيبة فقال «إنّه من هنا! من دمشق! إنّه لِصَديقَتي جوليا، أَتَمَنَّى أن يُعجِبها.» وسَأَلَه فادي لمن القُبَّعة المُلَوَّنة، فردّ جمال «لِنانسي. إنها من القُطن المصريّ. أَعتَقِد أنّها سَتَفرَح بِها. وفي شرم الشيخ اِشتَرَيتُ تي شيرت بُرتُقاليّ لِجاك، والأزرَق لِجورج، والأخضَر لِستيفن، أتمنّى أن تكون المَقاسات مُناسِبة لَهُم.»

إعداد *preparation*
أسعار *prices*
قُرط *earrings*
مُلَوَّن *multicolored*
أعتَقِد *I think/I believe*
سَتَفرَح *she will be happy*
مَقاسات *sizes*
مُناسِبة *suitable*

قالَت بهيجة إنّهم سَيَفرَحون جدّاً بهذه الهَدايا.

ورَدَّ جمال، «أَكيد! ومعي أيضاً طاولة الزهر بالصَدَف لِداني. هذه الحَلَوِيّات الشاميّة لأمّي وأبي.»

أكيد *for sure!*
حَلَويّات *candy/cakes*
شاميّة *Shami/Syrian*

«أنا كنتُ أودّ أن أبقى لِفَترة أطوَل وأزور أماكِن أكثر. أخذتُ صُوَراً كثيرة سَتُساعِدني على تَذَكُّر هذه الرحلة، ولكن أكيد أنا لَن أنساها.»

لَن أنساها *I will not forget it*

After reading بعد القراءة

A Test your understanding.

1 Jamal thinks that, compared to America, the prices in the Middle East are...

a about the same. b more expensive. c less expensive.

2 The earrings Jamal bought are made of...

a silver. b gold. c copper.

3 The hat is made of...

a Egyptian wool. b Egyptian silk. c Egyptian cotton.

4 In Sharm El-Sheikh Jamal bought a lot of...

a sandals. b postcards. c T-shirts.

5 During his trip Jamal took...

a a few photos. b a lot of photos. c no photos.

B Fill out the table with the details of the gifts Jamal is taking back with him.

Recipient	Gift
Julia	
Nancy	
Jack	
George	
Stephen	
Danny	
his parents	

Review 4

المراجعة ٤

في صَحراء سيناء رأى جمال مَلابِس البَدو البَيضاء الواسعة وملابس السيّدات السَّوداء الواسعة أيضاً.

وفي دَير «سانت كاثرين» اِتَّفَقَ جمال مع شابَّين من السويد، وآخر من الأرجنتين، وفَتاتَين من اِسكتلندا على أن يَستَيقِظوا معاً بعد مُنتَصَف اللَّيل لِيَتَسَلَّقوا الجَبَل لِمُشاهَدة شُروق الشَّمس من فوق القِمّة.

وفي شرم الشيخ اِشتَرَى جمال ملابس كثيرة مُلَوَّنة لأصدِقاءه في كاليفورنيا قبل أن يأخذ طائرة مصر للطَّيران إلى القاهرة لِزِيارة الأهرام.

قضى جمال في مِنطَقة الأهرام حوالي ساعة. رَكِبَ جَمَلاً اسمه منصور في جَولة قَصيرة وأَخَذَ صُوَراً كثيرة للأهرام وأبو الهول. ثمّ عاد إلى دمشق في المساء.

وحين جاء وقت إعداد الحقيبة، قال جمال لخالته إنّه كان يودّ أن يَبقَى لِفَترة أطول وأن يزور أماكِن أكثر، ولكنّه أخذ صُوَراً كثيرة سَتُساعِده على تَذَكُّر هذه الرحلة التي لَن يَنساها.

Vocabulary review مُراجَعة المُفرَدات

Across

3 شافة (3)

4 ثَلج (3)

6 اِتَّفَقتُ (1,6)

7 دَقيقة (6)

11 مُناسِب (8)

14 الأهرام (3,8)

18 مِصر (5)

19 سائِح (7)

Down

1 مُدَوَّنة (4)

2 أصدِقاء (7)

5 القاهِرة (5)

8 دَير (9)

9 مُنتَصِف اللَّيل (8)

10 ملابِس (7)

12 اِشترى (2,6)

13 أسعار (6)

15 السويد (6)

16 قُبَّعة (3)

17 أنف (4)

Part Two
الجزء الثاني

Arab Characters

شَخصيّات عَرَبيّة

1 Ahmed Shawqi Language and Historical Notes

- شاعِر = poet (plural = شُعَراء); شِعر = poetry/poem (plural = أشعار); linguistic prowess generally, and the ability to write poetry specifically, have been highly valued in Arab culture for centuries
- مَرموق = well-regarded, lofty
- المُجتَمَع = society
- قُرون = centuries (singular = قَرن)
- مَوهِبة = talent
- تَقدير = appreciation
- اِحتِرام = respect
- لَقَب = title, nickname
- زُمَلاءه الشُّعَراء = his fellow poets
- في أوائِل... = in the early stages ("beginnings") of...
- مَنزِلة خاصّة = a special standing
- تَرَبَّى = he was brought up

أحمد شوقي

الشاعِر لَهُ مَركَز مَرموق في المُجتَمَع العربيّ لأنّ العرب أحبّوا الشِّعر منذ قُرون، ونَظَروا لِمَوهِبة الشاعر بِنَظرة اِحتِرام وتَقدير. «أَمير الشُّعَراء» هو لَقَب حَصَلَ عليه أحمد شوقي من زُمَلائه الشُّعَراء في أوائِل القَرن العَشرين. ورُبَّما كان التَّقدير الآتي من الزُّمَلاء له مَنزِلة خاصّة.

كان أبوه من العراق وأمّه أُصولها تُركيّة مع يونانيّة. تَرَبّى في القَصر المَلَكيّ بالقاهرة لأنّ جَدّته كانَت تَعمل فيه.

أحمد شوقي (على اليَسار) مع الزَّعيم المصريّ، سَعد زَغلول

- في سِنّ مُبَكِّرة = at an early age
- القانون = law
- الأدَب = literature
- تِمثال = statue (plural = تَماثيل)
- مَسرَحيّات = plays (singular = مَسرَحيّة);
  مَسارِح = theaters (singular = مَسرَح)
- بِميزانيّات ضَخمة = with huge budgets
- قَصائِد = odes (singular = قَصيدة)
- أحزان وأفراح = sorrows and joys
- سِياسة = politics; سِياسيّ = political/politician
- تَمَّ نَفيه = he was exiled

Ahmed Shawqi **Test your understanding.**

1 What did Ahmed Shawqi's fellow poets call him?
2 What were the ethnic origins of his father and mother?
3 Where exactly was Ahmed Shawqi brought up and why?
4 What is Shawqi's house now used for?
5 Where are the two statues of the poet mentioned in the text?
6 To which country was Shawqi exiled and why?
7 How did Shawqi spend his time in exile?

ظَهَرَت مَوهِبَته في سِنّ مُبَكِّرة. وفي شَبابه، أَرسَلَه القَصر إلى فَرَنسا لِيَدرُس القانون. كما قامَ بِدِراسة الأَدَب الفرنسيّ أيضاً. أحبّ القِراءة في التاريخ والأدب.

بَيته في القاهرة قَصر أبيَض جَميل يُطِلّ على نَهر النيل. هذا القصر هو الآن مَتحَف فيه بعض الأوراق والكُتُب الخاصّة بِهِ وأشعار مَكتوبة بِخَطّ يَده. لِشوقي تِمثال من البرونز في الحَديقة، كما أن له تِمثال آخَر في حَديقة «بورجيزي» في روما، وهي حَديقة مَشهورة بِما فيها من المَتاحِف والمَعارِض واللَوحات الفَنّيّة والتَماثيل.

كَتَبَ أحمد شوقي مَسرَحيّات كامِلة من الشِّعر، عُرِضَت على مَسارِح مصر بِمُمَثِّلين مَشهورين وبِميزانيّات ضَخمة. كما كَتَبَ قَصائِد الشِّعر في الدين وفي حُبّ الوَطَن وفي أحزان وأفراح المُجتَمَع المصريّ والعربيّ من حَوله.

كما كَتَبَ في السِّياسة أيضاً. كِتابة الشعر في مَوضوعات سِياسيّة سَبَّبَت له مَشاكِل كثيرة مع القَصر المَلَكيّ والحُكومة البِريطانيّة وَتمَّ نَفيه إلى أسبانيا، فَقَضَى فيها عِدّة سَنَوات. هناك، تَعَلَّمَ اللُّغة الأسبانيّة وقامَ بِدِراسة آثار الحَضارة الإسلاميّة في الأَندَلُس.

2 Haroun Al-Rashid Language and Historical Notes

- Dates are often expressed using two different calendars:
  الميلاديّة or للميلاد ("Christian"), abbreviated to م; the Gregorian calendar familiar throughout the world
  الهِجريّة ("flight"), abbreviated to هـ; the lunar Islamic calendar, which starts at the year 622 AD with the prophet Mohammed's flight from Mecca to Madina. The date ١٧٠هـ is 170 (lunar) years after this flight.

- خَليفة = caliph (plural = خُلَفاء); = خِلافة caliphate

- عَبّاسيّ = Abbasid; العَصر العَبّاسي = the Abbasid era; the Abbasid caliphs ruled a large Islamic empire from their base in modern-day Iraq for much of the early Middle Ages

- اِشتَهَر بـ = [he] was famous (for)

- كان يُشَجِّع = [he] encouraged/was encouraging

- أَهل العِلم = people of knowledge; أَهل is also used for family members; the greeting أَهلاً suggests welcoming someone to a family-like group

- حِكمة = wisdom

- أَنشَأَ = [he] founded

- دور = role

- مُؤَسَّسات خَيريّة = charitable foundations

- حَفر آبار الماء = digging water wells

هارون الرشيد

الخَليفة هارون الرَّشيد هو خامس الخُلَفاء العَبّاسيّين في بَغداد بين ٧٦٣ و ٨٠٩م (١٧٠ و ١٩٣هـ).

اِشتَهَرَ هارون الرشيد بِأنّه كان يُشَجِّع العِلم والعُلَماء، والأدَب والأدَباء، والشِّعر والشُّعَراء، والتَّرجَمة والمُترَجمين، واللُّغات واللُّغويّين، والفَنّ والفَنّانين، والهَندَسة والمُهَندِسين، وغَيرهم من أهل العِلم والمَعرِفة والحِكمة في ذلك الوقت.

أَنشَأَ هارون الرشيد «بَيت الحكمة» في بغداد وجَمَعَ فيه أَفضَل العُقول. كما كان لِهارون الرشيد أيضاً دور كبير في أعمال الخَير، والمُؤَسَّسات الخَيريّة لِخِدمة الناس، مثل حَفر آبار الماء وبِناء بُيوت للفُقَراء.

- مَنارة = beacon, lighthouse
- مَثيل = [anything] comparable
- مُؤَرِّخون = historians
- قائِد بارِع = skillful leader
- السَّيطَرة على = control over
- شُعوب = peoples (singular = شَعب); قَبائِل = tribes (singular = قَبيلة); طَوائِف = factions (singular = طائِفة)
- دَخل = income; ثَراء = wealth
- ضَرائِب = taxes (singular = ضَريبة)

Haroun Al-Rashid **Test your understanding.**

1 When was the caliphate of Haroun Al-Rashid?
2 Can you find the specific words on page 73 that mean "poets," "translators," "artists," linguists," "literary figures," "engineers," "scientists/learned men"?
3 What was the name of the establishment where Haroun Al-Rashid gathered all these minds together?
4 How far did the Abbasid state extend under Haroun Al-Rashid?
5 What were his outstanding attributes as caliph?
6 How did the Abbasid state become rich under his rule?

في عَصره أَصبَحَت بغداد مَنارة لِلعِلم وأيضاً للحِرَف اليَدَويّة والصِّناعات التَقليديّة ونَشَطَت التِّجارة وتَحَوَّلَت الدَّولة العَبّاسيّة إلى دَولة كبيرة لم يكن لها مَثيل.

كان هارون الرشيد شابّاً عُمره حوالي ٢٥ سنة حين أَصبَحَ الخَليفة على دَولة كبيرة واسِعة تَمتَدّ من وَسَط آسيا شَرقاً حتى المُحيط الأَطلَنطيّ غَرباً . المُؤَرِّخون قالوا إن فَترة خِلافته كانت هي العَصر الذَهَبيّ للدَّولة العَبّاسية التي اِستَمَرَّت نحو خمسة قُرون.

كما قال بعض المُؤَرِّخين الآخَرين إنّه كان قائِداً بارِعاً للجَيش. وقالوا إنّه كان سِياسيّاً مَوهوباً لأنّه تَمَكَّنَ من السَّيطرة على مَساحات شاسِعة فيها شُعوب وقَبائِل وطَوائِف مُختَلِفة. وبِسَبَب قُوّة الدَّولة، زادَت الضَّرائِب، وزاد الدَّخل، ولا يَزال عَصر هارون الرشيد هو العَصر الذي يُستَخدَم كَمِثال لِثَراء الدَّولة.

3 Omm Kalthoum Language and Historical Notes

- قَريـة = villages (plural =قُرىً)
- مُؤَذِّن = muezzin; the man assigned to call for prayer; this is performed five times every day at different times, but the wording of the call is the same
- حِفظ = learning by heart, memorizing
- الأغـاني الديـنيّـة = religious songs
- وهـي تُغَنِّي = while she [was] singing
- تَـأَكَّدَ = [he] was certain
- جِسم = body, frame

أمّ كلثوم

وُلِدَت أمّ كلثوم عام ١٨٩٨ لأسرة فقيرة في قَرية صغيرة في ريف مصر. كان أبوها، الشَّيخ إبراهيم، هو مُؤَذِّن القرية. وفي يوم من الأيام، كان الشيخ إبراهيم يُحاوِل أن يُساعِد اِبنه خالِد على حِفظ بعض الأَغاني الدينيّة. وفَجأةً سَمِعَ اِبنَته الصُغرى وهي تُغَنِّي هذه الأغاني بِصَوت جَميل وقَويّ رغم أن عُمرها كان حوالي ستّ سَنَوات فَقَط. هنا تَأَكَّدَ الشيخ أن هناك مَوهِبة كبيرة داخل هذا الجِسم الصغير.

- أعياد = Eids, religious holidays (singular = عيد)
- أجر زَهيد = a nominal fee
- أعباء الحَياة = "the burdens of living," specifically expenses
- اِنبَهَروا = they were dazzled
- مُجاوِر = neighboring, adjacent
- اِنتَقَلَت الأُسرة = the family moved
- الطَّبَقات العُليا = upper layers; here used to mean "upper layers of society" or "upper classes"; can also be used in geology for layers of the earth or atmospheric strata, and in music for the higher octaves; كَثير الطَّبَقات = multilayered
- شُهرَتها = her fame
- اِختِراع = invention
- اِنتِشار = spread, dissemination

بعد ذلك بَدَأت أمّ كلثوم تُغَنّي في أعياد القَرية، وكانَت تَحصُل على أَجر زَهيد تُساعِد به الأسرة على مُواجَهة أعباء الحَياة. سَمِعَها الناس فانبَهَروا بِمَوهِبَتها وأَصبَحَت مشهورة ومطلوبة في قَريَتها وفي القُرَى المُجاوِرة والمُدُن القَريبة. وبعد أن كَبُرَت قَليلاً، كانَت تَقِف على المَسرَح وتُغَنّي بِمَلابِس الصِّبيان حتى لا يَعرِف الناس أنّها بنت.

وبعد فِترة، اِنتَقَلَت الأسرة إلى القاهرة، وغَنَّت أمّ كلثوم لِطَبَقات المُجتَمَع العُليا في القُصور وزادَت شُهرَتها كثيراً مع اِختِراع الراديو، ووَصَلَ صَوتها الجميل إلى مَلايين المُستَمِعين في مصر والعالَم العربيّ كلّه. وكَذلك، مع اِنتِشار التِليفِزيون، زادَت شُهرَتها أكثر وأكثر لأن المَلايين شاهَدوها على شاشاتهم وهي تُغَنّي على المَسرَح.

تِمثال أمّ كلثوم في القاهِرة

- كانَت تَتَمـايَل = she used to sway
- إحسـاس عَميق = profound emotion
- تَسجيلات حفَلاتـها = recordings of her concerts
- القَنَوات الفَضـائيّة والأرضيّة = satellite and terrestrial channels
- فِرقَتـها = her band
- أنيقة وحَريصة على مَظهَرهـا = elegant and mindful of her appearance
- يَدهـا اليُمنَى = her right hand
- مُجَوهَرات = jewels
- هِلال كَبير من المـاس = a large diamond crescent
- ضَئيل = slight, tiny

Omm Kalthoum **Test your understanding.**

1 Where and when was Omm Kalthoum born?
2 What was her father's role in the village?
3 How old was Omm Kalthoum when her father realized her talent?
4 What disguise did she wear on stage when she was young?
5 What two inventions increased her fame?
6 What did Omm Kalthoum always hold in her right hand while singing?
7 What details of Omm Kalthoum's appearance does the text mention?

حين كانَت أمّ كلثوم تُغَنّي، كانَت تَتَمايَل مع الموسيقَى وتُغَنّي بِإحساس عَميق. تَسجيلات حَفلاتها تُذاع إلى اليوم على القَنَوات الفَضائيّة والأرضيّة في كلّ البِلاد العربيَة. في مُعظَم تَسجيلات حَفلاتها المَوجودة، نَرَى أمّ كلثوم تَقِف في وَسَط المَسرَح وفِرقَتها الموسيقيّة وَراءَها، وفُستانها دائِماً أنيق وفي يَدها اليُمنَى مِنديل. كان لها بعض المُجَوهَرات المَشهورة تَرتَديها في الحَفلات، أَشهَرها هِلال كبير من الماس.

كانَت أمّ كلثوم سَيِّدة أَنيقة وحَريصة على مَظهَرها في الأماكِن العامّة. شَعرها كان أسوَد داكِناً كاللَّيل وكَثيفاً جدّاً. يَداها وقَدَماها كانَت صَغيرة وجِسمها ضَئيل رغم أن صَوتها كان قَويّاً كَثير الطَّبَقات.

4 Ibn Battuta Language and Historical Notes

- المَعروف بِـ = known as

- طَنجة = Tangiers; المَغرِب = Maghreb (literally "place where the sun sets," i.e., the west); this refers to the northwest of Africa, and is also the Arabic name for modern-day Morocco

- Mecca (مكّة) and Medina (المَدينة) are two cities in western Saudi Arabia, in the area known as Hijaz (الحِجاز). They have a special religious significance in Islam. Mecca is home to the holy shrine, the Ka'ba (الكَعبة), and it is where Muslims go for the annual pilgrimage known as Hajj (الحَجّ). It is the duty of every able Muslim to "perform the obligation of the pilgrimage" (يُؤَدّي فَريضة الحَجّ) at least once in his or her lifetime. Medina is where Prophet Muhammad is buried.

- قام بِها = [which] he undertook

- اِستَمَرَّت رِحلاته = his journeys continued/lasted

- الجَزائِر = Algeria

- آسيا الوُسطَى = central Asia

- خَطَر = danger

اِبن بطوطة

وُلِدَ شَمس الدين محمّد بن عبد الله الطَّنجيّ، المَعروف بِابن بَطوطة، في مدينة طَنجة في المَغرِب في القَرن الرابِع عشر الميلاديّ. وفي شَبابه، قَرَّرَ أن يُسافِر إلى الحِجاز لِيَزور المدينة ولِيُؤَدّي فَريضة الحَجّ في مَكّة.

كان ابن بطوطة في ذلك الوقت شابّاً عُمره حوالي عِشرين عاماً، وكانَت هذه أوَّل رِحلة قام بِها خارِج المغرب ولكنّها لم تَكُن الأخيرة. اِستَمرَّت رِحلاته حوالي ثلاثين عاماً زار فيها أكثر من أربعين بَلَداً وعادَ بعدها إلى المغرب لِيُصبِح رَجُلاً مَشهوراً.

في البِداية، اِتَّجَهَ ابن بطوطة شَرقاً ،نحو الجَزائِر ثمّ تونِس وليبيا حتى وصل إلى مصر، ومنها اِتَّجَهَ إلى فِلَسطين وسوريا، ثم اِتَّجَهَ جَنوباً إلى المملكة العربيّة السعوديّة لِيزور مكّة والمدينة. اِمتَدَّت رحلات ابن بطوطة بعد الحجّ، فزار الهِند والصين وبعض دُوَل آسيا الوُسطَى وإفريقيا.

في ذلك الوقت، كانت هذه الرِّحلات مُغامَرات حَقيقيّة وفيها الكثير من الخَطَر والصُّعوبة.

- الدَّفع الرُّباعيّ = four-wheel drive
- شاحِنات =trucks (singular = شاحِنة)
- مُعَدّات = equipment
- تَأشيرات دُخول وخُروج = entry and exit visas
- هَواتف مَحمولة = cell phones, mobile phones (singular = هاتِف مَحمول) ; also known as موبايل ,خَلَويّ ,هاتِف جَوّال
- لِتَتَّصِل = [in order] to contact
- الشُّرطة = the police
- هاجَمَك = attacked you
- لُصوص = thieves (singular = لِصّ)
- الإسعاف = ambulance
- لَو تَعَرَّضتَ لِحادِث = if you suffered an accident
- حُجوزات = reservations
- دَرّاجات بُخاريّة = motorbikes

كانت هذه الرِّحلات مُغامَرات حَقيقيّة

لا سيّارات بالدَّفع الرُّباعيّ لِتَعبُر بها الصَّحراء، ولا شاحِنات لِتَحمِل الماء والطَّعام والمُعَدّات. لا طائِرات ولا قِطارات. لا حُدود دُوَليّة ونُقَط عُبور وجَوّازات سَفَر وتَأشيرات دُخول وخُروج. لا هَواتَف مَحمولة لِتَتَّصِل بالشُّرطة لو هاجَمَك اللُّصوص أو لِتَتَّصِل بالإسعاف لو تَعَرَّضتَ لِحادِث. ولا إنَترنَت لِتَعرِف الأخبار. ولا حُجوزات في فَنادِق أو مَطاعِم ولا تَأجير لِسيّارات أو دَرّاجات بُخاريّة.

- مِلاحة = navigation; from the same root as مِلح (salt) and مَلّاح (sailor/navigator)
- تُشرِق وتَغرُب = rise and set
- خَطّ سَيرك = your route (literally, "the line of your walking")
- واحات = oases (singular = واحة)
- يَمتازون بِـ = distinguished by; characterized by
- الكَرَم وحُسن الضِّيافة = kindness and hospitality
- قَوافِل = convoys, caravans (singular = قافِلة)
- حَمير = donkeys (singular = حِمار); بِغال = mules (singular = بَغل)

Ibn Battuta **Test your understanding.**

1 Where and when was Ibn Battuta born?
2 How old was he when he started to travel?
3 In what order did Ibn Battuta visit these countries?
China, Syria, Tunisia, Libya, Egypt, Algeria, Saudi Arabia, India
4 Name three conveniences available to modern travelers that were not available to travelers in Ibn Battuta's time?
5 What did travelers in the time of Ibn Battuta use for navigation?
6 What means of transportation does the text mention were used by pilgrims in the time of Ibn Battuta?

ولكن كان هناك نُجوم تَسطَع في السَّماء لَيلاً ويُمكِنك أن تَستَخدِمها في المِلاحة، وشَمس تُشرِق وتَغرُب في نَفس الاِتِّجاه كلّ يوم ويُمكِنك أن تَستَخدِمها في تَحديد خَطّ سَيرك. وكان هناك واحات على الطَّريق، ومُدُن وقُرَى فيها سُكّان يَمتازون بالكَرَم وحُسن الضِّيافة.

في رحلات الحَجّ تَحديداً، كان هناك قَوافِل من آلاف المُسلِمين تَتَّجِه إلى مكّة في مَوسم الحجّ. اِستَخدَم المُسافِرون الجِمال والحَمير والبِغال والخَيل أو اِتَّجَهوا إلى مكّة سَيراً على الأقدام مع القَوافِل.

5 Mai Ziyada Language and Historical Notes

- تَعتَبِر نَفسها = considered herself [to be]
- ظاهِرة ثَقافيّة = a cultural phenomenon
- في مَجالات كَثيرة = in many fields
- ديوان = anthology, collection
- اِسم مُستَعار = assumed name

مي زيادة

مي زيادة (١٨٨٦ – ١٩٤١م) كانَت تَعتَبِر نَفسها فِلَسطينيّة ولُبنانيّة ومِصريّة، ولذلك قالوا عَنها إنّها ظاهِرة ثَقافيّة في العالَم العربيّ. كانَت سيّدة مَوهوبة في مَجالات كَثيرة. في اللُّغات، دَرَسَت اللاتينيّة والألمانيّة والأسبانيّة والإيطاليّة، وعَمِلَت كَمُدَرِّسة للإنجليزيّة كما كانَت تُعطي دُروساً في اللُّغة الفَرَنسيّة لأولاد الطَّبَقات العُليا في مصر. كانَت أيضاً شاعِرة كَتَبَت بالفرنسيّة وصَدَرَ لها ديوان اِستَخدَمَت فيه اِسماً مُستَعاراً.

الأديبة المشهورة، مي زيادة

- الإبداع = creativity, originality
- رِوايات = novels (singular = رِواية); خُطَب = speeches (singular = خِطاب); مُحاضَرات = lectures (singular = مُحاضَرة); أبحاث = studies, research [papers] (singular = بَحث)
- إتقان = her command/mastery
- تَحسين أُسلوبها في الكِتابة = improve her writing style
- الفَلسَفة = philosophy
- مؤَلِّفون = writers, authors
- مُفكِّرون = thinkers

Mai Ziyada **Test your understanding.**

1 What combination of nationalities did Mai consider herself to be?
2 Which languages did she study, and which did she teach?
3 How did she become famous?
4 What did she study in order to improve her grasp of Arabic language and writing style?
5 What instrument did she play?
6 Where did Mai set up her literary salon?
7 What day of the week was the salon held?

وكـانَـت مـي زيـادة مَـوهـوبـة في الأَدَب وتَـقـرَأ كَثيراً. كَتَبَت في المَجَلاّت الأَدَبيّة، واشتَهَرَت كِتاباتـها بما فيـها من الإبداع. كَتَبَت الرِوايات والخُطَب والمُحاضرات والأبحاث الـتـي نُـشِرَت في الجَرائِد والمَجَلاّت. عَمِلَت كَصَحافيّة ومُتَرجِمة إلى جانِب عَمَلها كَأَديبة. وحين أرادَت أن تَزيد من إتقانها للُّغة العربيّة وتَحسين أُسلوبها في الكِتابة دَرَسَت الفَلسَفة والتاريخ الإسلاميّ والأدب العربيّ.

كان صَوتها جميلاً في إلقاء الخُطَب والتكَلُّم وَسَط الناس كما أنّها كانَت تُجيد العَزف على البِيانو. وبعد أن أَصبَحَت نَجمة من نَجمات المُجتَمَع الأَدَبيّ، كان لها صالون أدبيّ مَشهور في القاهرة يَجتَمِع فيه الأَدَباء والشُّعَراء والمُؤَلِفون والمُفَكِّرون أيّام الثُّلاثاء.

Part Three
الجزء الثالث

Ali Baba and the Forty Thieves

علي بابا والأربعين حرامي

"Ali Baba and the Forty Thieves" is one of the famous stories from *One Thousand and One Nights*.

But what if Ali Baba were living among us now in this century? Let's take a look...

«علي بابا والأربعين حرامي» قصّة مشهورة من قصص «ألف ليلة وليلة».

ولكن، ماذا لو كان علي بابا يعيش معنا الآن في هذا القرن؟ تعالوا نرى...

Chapter 1 Language and Culture Notes

- تَلّ العَسَل = Honey Hill; Ali Baba's hometown

- بَطَل = hero

- مُتَهالِك = run-down, shabby

- بِلا = without

- قِسم التَّحرير = editorial department; قِسم is the word generally used for a company or government department; also قِسم الشُّرطة = police station

- دار تلّ العسل للنَّشر والتَّوزيع = The Honey Hill Publishing & Distribution House; two functions that usually appear together

- رَسائِل القُرّاء = readers' letters; رَسائِل is the plural of رِسالة (letter), and قُرّاء is the plural of قارِئ (reader)

الفَصل الأوّل

في مدينة اسمها «تلّ العَسَل» يعيش بَطَل القِصّة، علي بابا. إنّه شابّ فَقير ويَسكُن مع أمّه وأبيه في شقّة صغيرة من غُرفتَين. الشقّة فوق سَطح عمارة قديمة مُتهالِكة فيها خمسة أدوار ولكنّها بلا مِصعد. ليس عنده سيّارة ويذهب إلى عَمَله ماشياً.

علي بابا يعمل كَمُوظّف بسيط في قِسم التَّحرير بدار نَشر كبيرة اسمها «دار تلّ العسل للنَّشر والتَّوزيع». وَظيفَته هي الرَدّ على كلّ رَسائِل القُرّاء.

يذهب علي بابا إلى عمله ماشياً

- أسئِلة = questions (singular = سُؤال)

- جَرائِد = newspapers (singular = جَريدة)

- رُكن الكابتن ريشة = Captain Reesha's Corner; a young man connected to sports may often be referred to as "captain"; ريشة is literally "feather" and وَزن الريشة is one of the weights in boxing and wrestling; رُكن = corner, also a boxing term

- الدكتور ياقوت أبو الذَّهَب = Dr. Yaqoot Abul Dhahab; ياقوت = sapphire; ذَهَب = gold

- عَروس = bride (plural = عَرائِس)

- باب (literally meaning "door") can also be used to refer to a column or section in a newspaper or magazine, and sometimes a chapter of a book

- الخالة نَرجِس = Aunt Narjis; نَرجِس = Narcissus; نرجسيّ = selfish, narcissistic

- رَسّامو الكاريكاتير = cartoonists, caricaturists; رَسّامون = drawers, illustrators; the ن of the plural ending has disappeared because the word is in an *idaafa* construction ("drawers of the caricatures")

القرّاء يُرسِلون مَشاكِلهُم وأَسئِلَتهُم بالبريد العاديّ أو بالإيميل إلى مَجلاّت وجَرائِد الدار. علي بابا يَستَخدِم اسماً مُختَلِفاً حَسب نَوع المجلّة أو الجَريدة. مثلا، في مجلّة «أُسبوع تلّ العسل الرِّياضيّ» هو الكابتن ريشة، الذي يَرُدّ على القرّاء في «رُكن الكابتن ريشة».

وفي جريدة «التلّ الاِقتِصاديّ» هو الدكتور ياقوت أبو الذَهَب، الذي يَنصَح القرّاء في باب «أموالك مع أبو الذهب». وأمّا في مجلّة «عَروس تلّ العسل» فهو الذي ينصح العَرائِس في صَفحة «اسألوا الخالة نرجس».

علي بابا له مكتب صغير في ركن ضَيِّق من غرفة بلا شبّاك في الدور الأرضيّ. أمّا صاحِب الدّار، والمُديرون والصُحُفيّون الكِبار والكُتّاب المشهورون ورَسّامو الكاريكاتير المحبوبون فلَهُم مَكاتِب كبيرة مُكَيَّفة في الأدوار العُليا. مكاتبهم تُطلّ على الميدان الواسع والحديقة الخضراء والزهور المُلَوَّنة والنافورات. علي بابا يَقضي مَعظَم يومه على الاِنترنت، يُحاوِل أن يَجِد الإجابات الصَحيحة على أسئلة القرّاء لِيُساعدهُم على حَلّ مشاكلهم.

وفي يوم من الأيام، كان على بابا يقرأ البريد على الإيميل كَعادته. وفَجأةً عثر على رسالة غريبة مختلفة لأنّها بلا سؤال. بدأ على بابا في القِراءة:

سِرّيّ = secret, confidential; an adjective used a lot in an IT context: كَلِمة المُرور السِرّيّة = password; الرَّقم السِرّيّ = PIN ("secret number")

سِمسِم = sesame

المَبلَغ المُتاح لَك = the sum available to you; a commonly used banking term

تَحويل = transferring, forwarding (money, etc.)

حِساب = (bank) account

خُدعة = scam, deception

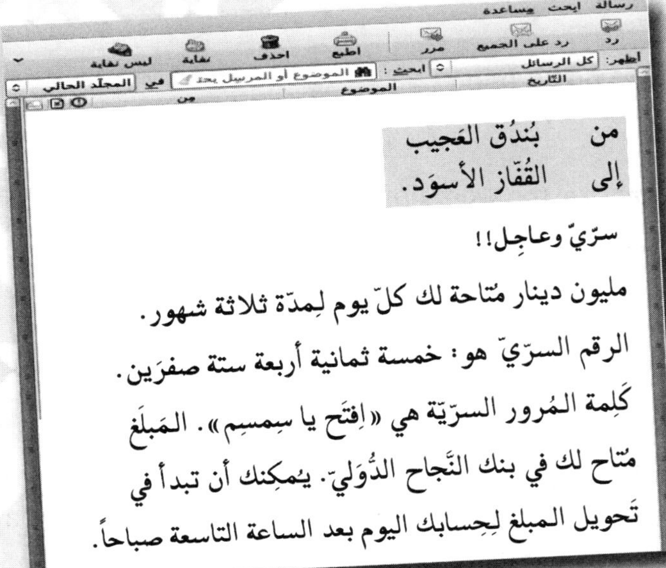
رسالة ابحث مساعدة

رد | رد على الجميع | مرر | اطبع | احذف | نفاية | ليس نفاية

أظهر: كل الرسائل ابحث: الموضوع أو المرسل يحتوي في المجلّد الحالي

التاريخ | الموضوع | من

من بُندُق العَجيب
إلى القُفّاز الأسوَد.

سرّيّ وعاجِل!!

مليون دينار مُتاحة لك كلّ يوم لِمدّة ثلاثة شهور.
الرقم السرّيّ هو: خمسة ثمانية أربعة ستة صفرَين.
كَلِمة المُرور السرّيّة هي «اِفتَح يا سِمسِم». المَبلَغ مُتاح لك في بنك النَّجاح الدُّوَليّ. يُمكِنك أن تبدأ في تَحويل المبلغ لِحسابك اليوم بعد الساعة التاسعة صباحاً.

نظر على بابا إلى شاشة الكمبيوتر وهو لا يُصَدِّق ما يَراه ويقرأه. «ما هذا الذي أراه وأقرأه؟ أنا لا أصدّق هؤلاء الناس. هل هذه خُدعة؟»

علي باب لا يصدّق ما يراه ويقرأه

- فـي ذِهـنـه = on his mind

- مَوقِع = website; the word literally means "position" or "site" but is the most common word in Arabic for website

- رايـات = banners

- سَمِـعَ أجراساً وصَفّارات وطُبولاً = he heard bells, whistles, and drums; a reference to the type of alert sounds you might hear on a computer

- سَحب = withdrawal (of money); to withdraw = سَحَبَ، يَسحَب

Chapter 1 Test your understanding.

1 How many rooms are there in the apartment where Ali Baba and his parents live?
2 How does Ali Baba get to work every day?
3 What is his job?
4 What three assumed names does Ali Baba use for his newspaper and magazine columns?
5 How much money does the mystery e-mail say is available daily?
6 What is the name of the bank where the account is held?
7 What is the PIN for the account?
8 What is the password?

مَرَّت لحظات وعلي بابا يَتَساءَل عن مَعنى هذا الكلام الغريب. «مَن هو بُندُق العَجيب؟ ما هذا القُفّاز الأسود؟ عن أي سمسم يَتَحَدَّثون؟ ماذا سَيَفتح هذا السمسم؟ مليون دينار كلّ يوم؟ أنا لا أفهم شيئاً.» قرّر علي بابا أن هذه الرسالة غير مَفهومة ومَليئة بالألغاز، فتركها وعاد إلى قراءة البريد الآخر.

ولكنّه عاد إلى هذه الرسالة نفسها بعد قليل وفي ذِهنه سؤال أو سؤالان أو ثلاثة أسئلة. سأل نفسه، «هل هذا ممكن؟ هل هذا معقول؟ سأُجَرِّب، وسَنَرى!» دخل علي بابا إلى مَوقع بنك النَّجاح الدَّولي، وأَدخَلَ الرقم السرّيّ الذي جاء في الرسالة: خمسة ثمانية أربعة ستة صفرَين، وكتب كلمة المرور السرّيّة «اِفتح يا سمسم!»

فجأةً ظَهَرَت على الشاشة رايات حمراء وخضراء وصفراء، وسمع أجراساً وصَفّارات وطُبولاً، وظهرت لَوحة على الشاشة تقول:

www.alnajahbank.com

مرحباً بك في بنك النجاح الدولي!

المبلغ المتاح لك اليوم هو...

مليون دينار

وإن كنت ترغب في سحب أو تحويل هذا المبلغ الآن

أَدخِل رقم الحساب هنا:

Chapter 2 Language and Culture Notes

- كوب من الشاي = a glass of tea; traditionally people would drink tea out of a glass, not a cup

- ظَلّ مُستَيقِظاً يُفكِّر = he stayed awake thinking

- رَصيد = (bank) balance

- آلة = a machine; the source of expressions that are related to automation: خِدمة الهاتِف الآليّة = automated phone service; آلة الصَرف الآليّ = automated teller machine (ATM)

- تَعليمات مُسَجَّلة = recorded instructions

الفَصل الثاني

في هذه الليلة، لم يَستطِع علي بابا أن ينام. حين قالَت أمّه «العشاء جاهِز يا علي!». قال لها «أنا لا أشعُر بالجوع يا أمّي.» وحين سَألَه أبوه «هل تريد كوباً من الشاي يا علي؟» ردّ عليه، «أنا لا أشعر بالعَطش يا أبي. ربّما ذهبتُ إلى غرفتي لأنام مُبَكِّراً.»

ولكن علي بابا في الحقيقة لم يَنَم مبكّراً، ولم ينم مُتَأَخِراً أيضاً، بل ظَلّ مُستيَقِظاً يُفَكِّر طَوال الليل فيما حَدَثَ له. وحوالي الساعة الخامسة صباحاً قرّر أن يَتَّصِل بِبنكه العادي، بنك تل العسل المحدود، ليعرف رَصيده.

أخذ هاتِفه المَحمول، وطلب رقم البنك، واِختار خِدمة الهاتِف الآليّة، ثمّ اِتَّبَع التَّعليمات المُسَجَّلة، فأدخَل رقم حِسابه، وتاريخ ميلاده، وسمع الصوت المُسَجَّل يقول، «رصيدك اليوم مِليون وتسعة وتسعون دينار فَقَط. شكراً لاستِخدامك هذه الخِدمة.» وبعدها سمع صوت صَفّارة طويلة.

قال علي بابا لِنَفسه، «هذا غير معقول! أنا أعرف أن رصيدي أمس صباحاً كان مِئة وتسعة ديناراً، وسَحَبتُ عشرة من آلة الصَرف الآليّ قبل أن أَتَناوَل الغداء. المفروض أن يكون رصيدي تسعة وتسعين ديناراً فقط، وليس مليون وتسعة وتسعين! هذا غير معقول! هل مَوضوع «افتح يا سمسم» هذا حقيقيّ؟»

- لم يُصَدِّق أُذُنَيه = he didn't believe his ears

- كَرَّر = repeated

- أفضَل وَسيلة للتَّأكُّد = the best way to be sure

- عُمَلاء = clients, customers (singular = عَميل);
contrast with عُمّال (singular = عامِل) later in the paragraph, from the same root but meaning "workers"

- سُلَّم = steps, stairs

- المَدخَل الرَّئيسيّ = the main entrance

- حَول قَدَمَيه = around his [two] feet; the ن of the dual ending has disappeared because the word has an attached pronoun (ه = his)

لم يُصَدِّق علي بابا أُذُنَيه وقَرَّرَ أن يَطلُب بنكه على هاتفه مرّة أُخرى، ولكنّ الصوت نفسه كَرَّرَ الكلام نفسه، والرصيد نفسه، ثم سمع الصفّارة الطويلة نفسها.

وهنا قرّر علي بابا أن أَفضَل وَسيلة للتَّأَكُّد من الرصيد مائة في المائة هي زِيارة سَريعة للبنك في الصباح.

عُمَلاء البنك كلّهم يَعرَفون أنّ البنك يَفتَح أبوابه الساعة التاسعة، ورغم ذلك كان علي بابا واقِفاً على سُلَّم المَدخَل الرئيسيّ الساعة الثامنة والثُلث. غَسَلَ عُمّال النَّظافة الصباحيّة سلّم المدخل من حول قَدَمَيه لأنّه رَفَضَ أن يتحرّك من مكانه على السلّم.

علي باب رفض أن يتحرّك من مكانه على السلّم

- صَرف = expenditure; the source of many words and expressions related to banking and fiscal activities: صَرّاف = bank teller; سِعر الصَّرف = exchange rate; مكتَب صَرّاف = currency exchange office; مَصرِف = bank; مَصروفات = expenses; مَصروف الجَيب = pocket money; see also ATM on page 102

- بِكلّ سُرور = with [all] pleasure

- إيصال = receipt; إيصال السَّحب = withdrawal slip

- الرَّصيد المُتَبَقّي = the remaining/outstanding balance

- نَهارك سَعيد! = "may your day be happy!"; the equivalent of "have a good day!"

- صَفّ واحد طَويل = one long line/row

- في المكان المُحَدَّد = in the designated place

Chapter 2 Test your understanding.

1 Why did Ali Baba call his bank at 5 AM?
2 What was the balance given to him by the automatic service?
3 What did he expect his balance to be?
4 How did he decide to make completely sure of his current balance after checking twice on the telephone?
5 What time did he arrive at his bank in the morning?
6 What did Ali Baba do as soon as he arrived at his office?

اِبتَسَم الصَّرّاف وقال، «صباح الخير. مرحباً بك في بنك تلّ العسل المحدود. أيّة خِدمة؟»

«صباح النور. أريد أن أسحَب مائة دينار من حسابي لو سَمَحت.»

«بكلّ سُرور. تفضّل. هذا هو المَبلَغ المَطلوب، وهذا إيصال السَّحب، ومكتوب فيه الرَّصيد المُتَبَقّي. نَهارك سَعيد!»

أخذ علي بابا المائة دينار والإيصال، واِتَّجَهَ إلى باب الخُروج وهو يَبتَسِم. الإيصال مكتوب فيه أرقام تسعة كثيرة جدّاً في صَفّ واحد طويل.

ورغم أنه لم يَنَم أمس، جَرى علي بابا إلى مكتبه الصغير في دار تلّ العسل للنشر والتوزيع، وجلس يُفَكِّر. وبعد قليل، قَرَّرَ أن يُجَرِّب شيئاً. فتح موقع بنك النجاح الدوليّ مرّة أخرى، واِتَّبَعَ الخَطَوات نفسها، وأدخل الرقم السرّيّ وكلمة المرور «اِفتح يا سمسم» فَظَهَرَت الرايات الملوَّنة وسمع الأجراس والصفّارات والطبول، فأدخل رقم حسابه الشخصيّ في المكان المُحَدَّد.

ثم اِنتَظَرَ خمس دَقائِق، وبعدها اِتَّصَلَ ببنكه، بنك تلّ العسل المحدود، وجاءَه نفس الصوت المُسَجَّل يقول، «رصيدك اليوم مليون وتسعمائة، تسعة وتسعون ألف، وتسعمائة، تسعة وتسعون دينار فقط. شكراً لاِستِخدامك هذه الخدمة.» وبعدها سمع صوت الصفّارة الطويلة.

Chapter 3 Language and Culture Notes

- حَدائِق = gardens (singular = حَديقة)

- بُحَيرة صَغيرة يَرسو فيها يَخت كَبير = a small lake on which a large yacht is moored

- مَلعَب = "place for playing" (plural = مَلاعِب); can be used simply to mean "playground" or "playing field" or for various sports: ملعب تَنس = tennis court; ملعب جولف = golf course; ملعب كُرة سَلّة = basketball court; ملعب كُرة القَدَم = soccer/football pitch

- حَجم = size; used in many expressions: حَجم أوليمبيّ = Olympic-sized; حَجم عائليّ = family-sized; مُتَوَسِّط الحجم = medium-sized

- غُرفة حَمام بُخار = steam room

- خُيول عَرَبيّة أصيلة = thoroughbred Arabian horses

- جَيش صَغير = a small army

- بُستانيّ = gardener

- مُدَرِّب خاصّ للياقة البَدَنية = private personal fitness trainer

- جيران = neighbors (singular = جار)

الفَصل الثالث

تَغَيَّرَت حَياة علي بابا تَماماً. في خِلال شَهر واحد جَمَعَ ثلاثين مليون دينار، مليون كلّ يوم، عن طريق «اِفتح يا سمسم»، كلمة المرور إلى عالَم جديد. فاِشتَرَى قَصراً كبيراً، في حَدائِقه الواسِعة بُحَيرة صغيرة يَرسو فيها يَخت كبير. وراء القصر مَلاعِب تَنِس عُشبيّة ومَلعَب جولف ومَلعَب كُرة سَلّة، وحَمّام سِباحة مَفتوح بالحَجم الأوليمبيّ لشُهور الصيف، وآخر مَسقوف بالمِياه الدافِئة لشُهور الشِتاء، وغرفة حمّام بُخار تركيّ، وساونا بالحجم العائِليّ مُستَورَدة من فِنلَندا، وسينما، وديسكو، وقاعة حَفَلات رَسميّة، وحَديقة حَيَوانات، واِسطَبل لخُيوله العربيّة الأصيلة.

وفي قصره كان هناك جَيشاً صغيراً من المُساعِدين والطَّبّاخين والبُستانيّين والسائِقين والنَجّارين وعُمّال النَّظافة، ومُدَرِّب خاصّ لِلياقة البَدَنيّة من السويد، وحلاّق فَرَنسيّ، ومدرّس بيانو إيطاليّ.

ولكن أَهَمّ نَجاح في حياته الجديدة كان «مُرجانة»، اِبنة جيرانه الجميلة. أحبّ علي بابا «مرجانة» عن بُعد مُنذُ أن كان صَبيّاً.

- تـاجِر خُضـار = vegetable merchant/trader
- سوق الـجُملة = wholesale market
- ملِكة جَمال = beauty queen
- أربَع سَنَوات مُتَتالِية = four years running
- رِسالة الماجِستير في إدارة الأعمال = Masters in Business Adminstration; the order of study in higher education is generally البكالوريوس (Bachelors/first degree), الماجستير (Masters), الدُكتوراه (Doctorate)
- مَلايين = millions (singular = مِليون)
- مَلأَته بالثِّقة والشُّجاعة = filled him with confidence and bravery
- تُدير كلّ شُؤون قَصره = run all the affairs of his palace
- على الفَور = immediately
- جَناح خاصّ = private wing; as in English, جَناح (plural أجنِحة) can be used for bird's wings, the wing of a building, or the wing of an organization, for example a political party

حين كان فقيراً، كان يَوَدّ أن يُقابِلها أو يَتَمَشّى معها في الحديقة أو أن يَدعوها إلى الغَداء معه، أو إلى السينما أو تَناوُل الشاي، ولكنّه كان يَخاف أن تَرفُض طَلَبه لأنّه فقير وهي ابنة تاجِر خُضار كبير في سوق الجُملة. كما أنّها فازَت بِلَقَب «مَلِكة جَمال تلّ العسل» أربع سنَوات مُتَتالِية، وصُوَرها موجودة في واجِهة صالون «مَدام نانسي» لِتَصفيف شَعر السيِّدات. لم تكن مرجانة جميلة فقط، ولكنّها كانت ذَكِيّة أيضاً، فكانت تُحَضِّر رسالة الماجستير في إدارة الأعمال من جامِعة تلّ العسل.

ولكن الآن، فإن مَلايين علي بابا مَلأَته بالثِّقة والشُّجاعة، فطلب منها أن تُدير كلّ شؤون قصره ومُوَظَّفيه وأملاكه ومَلايينه، فوافَقَت على الفَور. أَعطاها جَناحاً خاصّاً بها في قصره لِتكون قريبة من مكان عَمَلها.

صُوَر مُرجانة موجودة في صالون «مدام نانسي»

- أصبَحَ = became

- يَشغَل باله = troubled him (literally, occupied his mind)

- عَنيدة = stubborn

- تَنقيب = digging; often used in the context of mining or excavating; here used to mean digging around for information on the Internet

- مكتَبة عامّة = public library

هكذا أَصَبَحَ علي بابا هو أسعد شابٍّ في تلّ العسل، وخاصّةً حين تكون مرجانة بِجانِبه.

ولكن، كان هناك شَيء ما يَشغَل باله حين يذهب إلى سريره في المساء. مَن هو هذا البُندُق العَجيب؟ ما هو لُغز هذا القُفّاز الأسود؟ كيف وَصَلَت الأرقام وكلمة المُرور السرّيّة «اِفتح يا سمسم» إليه بهذه السُّهولة؟ مِن أين تَأتي كلّ هذه المَلايين، ومَن هو صاحِبها؟

طلب علي بابا من مرجانة أن تُساعِده في حَلّ هذه الألغاز. ولأنّها كانَت ذكيّة وماهِرة وعَنيدة، فإنّها حَصَلَت على مَعلومات مُفيدة بعد ساعات طويلة من البَحث والتَنقيب والدِراسة على الإِنترنت وفي مَكتَبة تلّ العسل العامّة.

كان هناك شيء ما يَشغَل باله حين يذهب إلى سريره

- عِصابة = gang, band, troop

- لُصوص = thieves (singular = لِصّ); although the title of the Ali Baba story uses حَرامي to mean "thief," لِصّ is the more standard term

- جِهاز شُرطة = police force; جِهاز = system, organization

- الأُمَم المُتَّحِدة = the United Nations (UN)

- سَرَقَت = stole

- مَخازِن = storage rooms, warehouses (singular = مَخزَن); the English "magazine" is derived from this Arabic word

- خِزانة فولاذيّة = a steel safe; steel = فولاذ

- اِسم الشُّهرة = *nom de guerre*, pyseudonym

- القِصَص التي نَسَجَها الناس = the stories people have woven

- بَصَمات الأصابِع = fingerprints

قالت مرجانة، : «اِجلِس هنا يا على بابا، واِستَمِع إلى ما سَأَقوله لك جَيِّداً. هناك عِصابة خَطيرة اسمها عِصابة القُفّاز الأسود، عَدَد اللُصوص فيها أربعون. هذه العِصابة مَطلوبة من سبعة وثلاثين جِهاز شُرطة حول العالم، كما أنّها مطلوبة من البنك الدُوَليّ، ومن الأُمَم المُتَحِدة، والبيت الأبيض في واشِنطُن، والاِنتَربول، وسكوتلاند يارد في لُندُن. سَرَقَت هذه العصابة نصف طُنّ من الذَهَب من البنك المَركَزيّ في جنوب اَفريقيا، وسرقَت عشر حَقائِب مَليئة بالماس من أحد المَخازِن في بَلجيكا، وسرقت مُجَوهَرات أُسرة حاكِمة في الخَليج، وسرقَت ثلاث لَوحات لِبيكاسو من خزانة فولاذيّة مَدفونة تحت قصر مِليونَير أمريكيّ في تكساس.»

اِعتَدَلَ علي بابا في مِقعَده وقال، «اِستَمِرّي يا مرجانة.»

فقالَت، «أمّا عن القفّاز الأسود نفسه، فهو اسم الشُّهرة لِرَئيس هذه العصابة. لا أحد يعرف من هو، ولا اسمه الحَقيقيّ، أو عُمره، أو مكان وِلادته، أو جِنسيّته، أو أين يُقيم. القِصَص التي نَسَجَها الناس حَوله كثيرة، بعضها حقيقيّ، وبعضها من الخِيال، وبعضها خَليط من الحقيقة والخيال معاً. مثلا، يقولون إنّ اسمه القفّاز الأسود لأنّه لا يَترُك بَصَمات أَصابِعه في مكان الجَريمة.»

اِعتَدَل علي بابا في مِقعَده مرّة ثانية وكَرَّرَ، «لا يَترُك بَصَمات أَصابِعه في مكان الجَريمة...»

- تـاجِر جلُود = a leather merchant

- حـاوَلَ أن يُرغِمَ اِبنـه = he tried to force his son

- عُقدة نَفسيّة = psychological complex; نَفس = self; نَفسيّ = psychological ("related to the self"); عِلم النَفس = psychology ("science of the self")

- أسلِحـة = weapons (singular = سِلاح)

- المُسَدَّسات والخَنـاجِر = pistols and daggers

- يَخنُق أعداءه = strangle his enemies

- يَده اليُسرَى = his left hand; يَده اليُمنَى = his right hand; يَد (hand) is feminine as are many parts of the body that appear in pairs

- لِيَمسَح عَرَقه = to wipe his sweat

Chapter 3 Test your understanding.

1 From where did Ali Baba bring the following for his new palace: steam bath; sauna; personal trainer; barber; piano teacher?
2 Who was Murjana, and what did she win four years running?
3 Why was Ali Baba afraid to approach Murjana in the past?
4 Murjana discovered that the gang leader, "The Black Glove," was wanted by 37 police forces and by which other organizations?
5 What examples did Murjana give of thefts the gang carried out?
6 What three theories did she relate to Ali Baba as to why the leader might be known as "The Black Glove"?

قالت مرجانة، «نعم، لا يترك بصمات أصابِعه. وهناك مَن يقولون أن اسمه القفّاز الأسود لأن أباه كان تاجِر جُلود كبير، وحاوَلَ أن يُرغِم اِبنه على العمل معه في تِجارة الجُلود. ولكن الاِبن كان يَكرَه رائِحة الجِلد، فَتَرَبَّت عنده عُقدة نَفسيّة وهو طِفل جَعَلَته يَتَّجِه إلى عالم الجريمة.»

وَقَفَ علي بابا ثمّ سارَ نحو الشبّاك وهو يُكَرِّر، «تَرَبَّت عنده عُقدة نفسيّة...»

واِستَمَرَّت مرجانة، «نعم، وهناك أيضاً مَن يقولون أن الاسم جاءَ لأنّه لا يَستَخدِم الأَسلِحة العاديّة مِثل المُسَدَّسات أو الخَناجِر، بل يحبّ أن يَخنُق أَعداءه بِيَدَيه.»

لَم يُكَرِّر علي بابا الجُزء الأَخير، بَل وَضَعَ يَده اليُسرَى على عُنُقه، وبِيَده اليُمنَى أَخرَجَ المِنديل من جَيبه لِيَمسَح عَرَقه.

Chapter 4 Language and Culture Notes

- زَميل = colleague, (work)mate (plural = زُمَلاء)

- اِشتِراك = subscription; مُشتَرِك = subscriber; تَحصيل الاِشتِراكات = collection of subscriptions

- فَخور بِهِ = proud of him

- أساليب سَخيفة = irritating methods; سَخيف is an adjective with negative connotations that can mean "annoying," "trivial," "silly," etc., depending on the context

- لِيَتَخَلَّصوا مِنه = to get rid of him

- صِلَة قَرابة بَعيدة = a distant kinship, i.e., they were distant relatives

- كان دائِماً يَتَجاهَله = always used to ignore him

- بَطاطا = "potatoes" or "sweet potatoes"; the name of Qasim's daughter

- هذا المَلعون = this accursed [man]

- حاسِب شَخصيّ = personal computer; حاسِب is a shorter version of آلة حاسِبة

الفَصل الرابع

«قاسم» هو زَميل على بابا في دار تلّ العسل للنشر والتوزيع، ولكنّه لا يعمل في التَحرير مِثله، بل في قِسم تَحصيل الاِشترِاكات. «قاسم» له مَهِمّة مُحَدَّدة في القسم وهي مُطارَدة المُشتَركين الذين يَتأَخَّرون في دَفع اِشترِاكاتهم. مُدير قسم التَّحصيل فَخور به لأنّ قاسم يَستَخدِم أَساليب سَخيفة مع المشتركين المُتَأَخِّرين، ودائِماً يَعود بالمال الكثير لأنّهم يُفضّلون أن يَدفَعوا الاشتراكات بِسُرعة لِيَتَخلَّصوا منه.

هناك صِلة قَرابة بَعيدة بين قاسم وعلى بابا، لكن قاسم كان دائماً يَتَجاهَله لأن علي بابا فَقير. ولكن، مُنذُ أن أَصبَحَ غَنياً، بَدَأَ قاسم يَطلُب علي بابا مَرّتَين أو ثلاث مَرّات يوميّاً على هاتفه المحمول، لِيَدعوه على العَشاء أو الغَداء أو الشاي أو القهوة أو لِحُضور عيد ميلاد اِبنته «بطاطا». قاسم الآن يقول للموظّفين في دار تلّ العسل للنشر والتوزيع: «علي بابا حَبيبي. أنا طَوال عُمري أحبّه مثل أخي تماماً، بل وأكثر من أخي أيضاً.»

ولكن في بيته، حين يجلس مع زوجته «أمّ بطاطا» يقول، «ماذا حَدَثَ لهذا المَلعون؟ من أين جاء بكلّ هذا المال؟ لابدّ أن هناك سرّ. آخ! كم أنا مُشتاق لِمَعرِفة السرّ! ولكن، هل لاحَظتِ يا أمّ بطاطا أن علي بابا يحمل الحاسِب الشَّخصيّ معه في كلّ مكان؟ حتى حين يَدخُل الحَمّام فهو يأَخُذه معه. هل لاحظتِ ذلك يا أمّ بطاطا؟»

- فِكرة جَهَنَّميّة = a devilish idea; جَهَنَّم = hell; جَهَنَّميّ = devilish, dastardly

- أحمَق! أعمَى! = Fool! Blind man!; i.e., "He must be a blind fool!" (to prefer Murjana to Batata)

- دَقَّت الجَرَس = she rang the bell

- بِدَهشة = with astonishment

- خَير؟ is an expression of surprise at something unexpected, hoping that it is good news

- على ما يُرام = alright, in order

- اِبتَلَعَت = she swallowed

- اِطمَئِني = relax, don't worry

- في المَنام = in a dream; مَنام = "place of sleep"

- فُستان أبيَض من الحَرير = a white silk dress; implying it is a good omen, perhaps resulting in a wedding soon

- البُنّ اليَمَنيّ الفاخِر وحَبّ الهال = fine Yemeni coffee beans and cardamom; Yemen is famous for growing coffee; cardamom is added for flavor

- نور عَيني = "light of my eye"; a term of endearment

فَرَدَّت عليه زَوجَته، «نعم، نعم لاحظتُ يا قاسم. لابدّ أن يكون السرّ في هذا الحاسب. أنا عندي فِكرة جَهَنَّميّة سَنَعرِف بها كلّ شيء. سَأَصِل إلى السرّ عن طريق الملعونة، مرجانة. أنا لا أعرف ماذا يَرَى فيها. اِبنَتنا بطاطا أَجمَل وأَذكَى منها. أَحمَق! أَعمَى!»

وفي اليوم التالي ذَهَبَت أمّ بطاطا إلى قصر على بابا في الصباح الباكر بعد الفَجر بِقَليل ودَقَّت الجَرَس. فَتَحَت مرجانة الباب وهي نصف نائمة، وقالت بِدَهشة، «أمّ بطاطا؟! صباح الخير! كم الساعة؟ خير؟ هل قاسم بخير؟ هل كلّ شيء على ما يُرام؟ هل بطاطا بخير، أم أنّها اِبتَلَعَت هاتفها المحمول مرّة أُخرى؟»

رَدَّت أمّ بطاطا، «اِطمَئِنّي يا حبيبتي، نحن كلّنا بخير، اطمئنّي. كلّ ما في الأَمر هو أنّني رَأَيتُك أمس في المَنام. كان حُلماً جميلاً! كنتِ تَلبَسين فُستاناً أبيض من الحَرير وفي يدك باقة زُهور بَيضاء! كما أنّني أُحِبّ قهوتك اللذيذة التي تُعَدِّينها بالبُنّ اليَمَنيّ الفاخِر وحَبّ الهال!» ضَحِكَت مرجانة وقالت، «أهلاً بك في أيّ وقت يا أمّ بطاطا! تَفَضَّلي. أنا سَأُعِدّ القهوة حالاً.»

جلسَت أمّ بطاطا في المطبخ مع مرجانة ونظرَت حولها فَرَأَت حاسب علي بابا الشخصيّ على المائِدة بِجوار الشُّبّاك. هذا هو رُكن على بابا المُفَضَّل في المطبخ. وبعد أن أَعَدَّت مرجانة القهوة قالت لها أمّ بطاطا «مرجانة يا حبيبتي، أَعتَقِد أنّني سمعتُ على بابا يُناديك يا نور عَيني.»

- سَأصعَد = I'll go up
- صينيّة = a tray
- كاميرا رَقميّة = digital camera; رَقم = number, digit; رَقميّ = digital
- دَسَّت الكاميرا بَين حلَّتَين كَبيرتَين = she slipped the camera between two large pots
- وَجَّهَتها نَحو = she directed it toward, she angled it toward
- كَبَسَت زِرّ التَّشغيل = she pressed the "on" button
- اِبتسامة البَراءة والرِّضا = the smile of innocence and contentment

رَدَّت مرجانة، «سَأَصعَد إلى غرفته حالاً وسآخذ له معي فِنجان من هذه القهوة الطازِجة.»

صَعَدَت مرجانة إلى الطابِق الأوَّل وهي تَحمِل صينيّة عليها كوب من عَصير البُرتُقال وفنجان قهوة لعلي بابا. وهنا، أَخرَجَت أمّ بطاطا من حَقيبتها كاميرا رَقميّة صغيرة تعمل بالبَطّاريّة، ووَقَفَت فوق كرسيّ خَشَبيّ ودَسَّت الكاميرا بين حلّتَين كَبيرتَين على رَفّ عالٍ ووَجَّهَتها نحو ركن علي بابا المفضّل، وكَبَسَت زِرّ التَّشغيل الأحمر الصغير.

وبعد ذلك عادَت أمّ بطاطا لتجلس على الكرسيّ، ورَسَمَت على وَجهها اِبتِسامة البَراءة والرِّضا.

دسّت الكاميرا بين حلّتين كبيرتين على رفّ عالٍ

- خَطَوات = [foot]steps

- رَشفة = a sip

- مِقدار فِنجانَين من = two cups worth of

- ...كان قاسِم وأمّ بَطاطا يَجلِسان = Qasim and Umm Batata were [both] sitting; the dual ending is added only to the verb after the subject; if the subject is put first, both verbs have the dual ending:
  ...إنّ قاسِم وأمّ بَطاطا كانا يَجلِسان

- ما تُسَجِّله وتَبُثّه الكاميرا = what the camera is recording and transmitting

- اُنقُر المَفاتيح = "strike the keys"; a way of saying "type" or "key"

- مُفلِس تَماماً = completely broke, completely penniless

حين سمعت أمّ بطاطا خَطَوات مرجانة وهي تَنزِل على السُّلَّم تَناوَلَت فنجانها وأخذَت رَشفة من القهوة اللذيذة، وقالت لها، «كم هي لذيذة هذه القهوة يا حبيبتي! سأترُكك الآن بعد أن اِطمَأَنَّ قَلبي. سآخذ مِقدار فنجانَين من البنّ معي لقاسم. أراك قريباً يا نور عيني.»

☕ ☕ ☕

وبعد نصف ساعة تقريباً، كان قاسم وأمّ بطاطا يجلسان في بيتهما جَنباً إلى جَنب أمام الكُمبيوتر في حُجرة النوم يَتابَعان ما تُسَجِّله وتَبُثّه الكاميرا من فوق الرَف. «أُنظُري يا أمّ بطاطا! انظري إلى الشاشة! يَبدو أن علي بابا يَدخُل إلى مَوقع بنك النجاح الدوليّ! يا أمّ بطاطا، بِسُرعة! هاتي وَرَقة وقَلَم واُكتُبي هذه الأرقام التي يَكتُبها: خمسة، ثمانية، أربعة، ستّة، صفر، صفر. عَظيم! والآن اكتبي هذه الحُروف: ألف، فاء، تاء، حاء، ياء، ألف، سين، ميم، سين، ميم.»

قالت أمّ بطاطا، «هَيَّا يا قاسم. أنقُر المَفاتيح مثل هذا الملعون لنرى ما سَيَحدُث.»

وبعد دَقائِق، أخذ قاسم هاتفه المحمول، وطلب بنكه لَمَعرِفة رَصيده رغم أنّه يعرف أن رصيده صِفر لأنّه مُفلِس تماماً، واِختار خِدمة الهاتف الآليّة، ثمّ اِتَّبَعَ التَّعليمات المُسَجَّلة ، فأَدخَلَ رقم حِسابه، وتاريخ ميلاده، وسمع الصوت المسجّل يقول، «رصيدك اليوم مليون دينار فقط.

⊛ بينَما = while, at the same time as

⊛ تُراقِبهُما وهي تلتَهِم = watching [both of] them while gobbling

Chapter 4 Test your understanding.

1 What specifically was Qasim's job in The Honey Hill Publishing & Distribution House?

2 How did Qasim's attitude toward Ali Baba change when he became rich?

3 Who are Batata and Umm Batata?

4 Why does Umm Batata secretly place a camera in Ali Baba's kitchen?

5 What does the camera record?

6 What do Qasim and Umm Batata do with the information?

شكراً لاستخدامك هذه الخدمة.» وبعدها سمع صوت صفّارة طويلة.

وبعد قليل، كان قاسم وأمّ بطاطا يَرقُصان في وَسَط الغرفة، بينما جلسَت بطاطا تُراقِبهُما وهي تَلتَهِم قِطعة شوكولاتة من الحَجم العائِليّ الكبير.

كان قاسم وأمّ بطاطا يرقصان في وسط الغرفة

Chapter 5 Language and Culture Notes

- بُندُق = hazelnut; a popular nickname for someone slight and/or nimble
- عَجيب = extraordinary, remarkable
- سَرِقة = theft; مَسروق = stolen
- تَزوير = forgery
- غَسيل الأموال = money laundering ("washing of monies")
- دون أن يَشعُر بالتَعَب أو بالمَلَل = without feeling tired or bored
- يَتَلاعَب = toying with; the basic verb يَلعَب simply means playing, whereas this form (VI) carries the meaning of playing confidently with something, as a cat would with a mouse
- تَلُفّ وتَدور = twisting and turning
- اِستِثمارات رَسميّة = legitimate/official investments

الفَصل الخامس

المحاسب، «بندق العجيب»

«بُـنـدُق الـعَـجيب» مُـحـاسِـب مـاهِـر جدّاً ولكنّـه أيضـاً لصّ كبير، له تاريخ طويل في السَّرِقة والتَّزوير. إلا أن جَريمَته المُفَضَّلة هي غَسيل الأموال لأنّه يَعتَقِد أنّها جريمة عالِية لا تُناسِب اللُصوص العاديّين. بندق العجيب يحبّ عَمَله كَلصّ، ويـجلس أمـام الكمـبيوتـر ساعة وراء ساعة دون أن يَشعُر بـالتَّعَب أو بـالمَلَل، يَتَلاعَب بـالملايين المَسروقة ويُحَوِّلـها إلى ملايين نَظيفة تَدخُل وتَخرُج وتَلُفّ وتَدور في اِستِثمارات رَسميّة.

- اِنضَمّ = joined
- مَوهبَته = his talent
- يَلمَع = shine
- صَعِدَ نَجمه = his star rose
- الذِّراع الأيمَن = "the right arm"; i.e., the right-hand man
- أن يُؤَدِّي لهُ = to perform for him
- تَغيير العُملات = exchange of currencies
- عَمَليّة = transaction (plural = عَمَليّات)
- يَستَطيع أن يُؤَدِّيها وهو نائِم = he can perform it while he is asleep
- قام بـِ = he undertook; a verb followed by the preposition بِ
- بِخَطأ بَسيط = through a simple error
- لَوحة = [key]board
- تَحديداً = specifically

مُنذُ سَنَوات قليلة، اِنضَمّ بندق العجيب إلى عَصابة القفّاز الأسود كلصّ بَسيط، ولكن مَوهَبَته جَعَلَته يَلمَع بين زُمَلائه اللُّصوص. وبسرعة صَعِدَ نَجمه في العصابة، إلى أن أصبح هو الذِّراع الأَيمَن لِلرَّئيس، القفّاز الأسود نفسه. كان القفّاز الأسود يطلب من بندق العجيب أن يُؤَدِّي له الخِدمات الماليّة، مثل التَّحويل بين الحِسابات، أو بيع وشِراء وتَغيير العُملات، أو السَّحب، والإيداع، والعَمَليّات المَصرِفيّة الأُخرى.

وفي يوم من الأيام، طلب القفّاز الأسود من بندق العجيب أن يفتح له حساباً سرّياً في بنك النجاح الدوليّ. هذه عَمَليّة سَهلة جدّاً بالنِّسبة لأيّ محاسب، أمّا بالنِّسبة لمحاسب في مَهارة بندق، فهي عمليّة يَستَطيع أن يُؤَدِّيها وهو نائِم، أو واقِف على رأسه، أو الاِثنان معاً.

قام بندق العجيب بالخَطَوات اللازِمة لِفَتح الحساب السرّيّ، ثمّ أرسل كلّ تَفاصيل الحساب إلى عُنوان القفّاز الأسود على الايميل. ولكن بندق، بِخَطَأ بَسيط على مَفاتيح لَوحة الكمبيوتر، أرسل هذه التَّفاصيل أيضاً إلى مَوقع مجلّة «عَروس تلّ العسل»، وتَحديداً، إلى باب «اِسألوا الخالة نَرجِس».

- نـاحِيـة أُخرى = another side
- تَصميم فَساتين العَرائِس = design of bridal dresses
- أوقـات الفِراغ = spare time, leisure time
- أفراح = weddings (singular = فَرَح)
- زَخرَفة = decoration, ornamentation
- أمتـار = meters (singular = مَتر)
- بـالصُّدفة = by coincidence
- العَدَد الأُسبوعيّ = the weekly issue; عَدَد = number or quantity; in this context it means "issue" of the magazine

Chapter 5 Test your understanding.

1 What is the function of "Bunduq al-Ajeeb" in the gang?
2 What is his favorite crime and why?
3 What is his secret hobby?
4 Which magazine does he read for information about his hobby?
5 How did Bunduq end up sending the details of the secret bank account to Ali Baba?

باب «اسألوا الخالة نرجس»؟ نعم! فَهناك ناحِية أُخرى لِشَخصيّة بندق العجيب لا يعرفها أحد. بندق العجيب عنده هِواية غَريبة بالنِّسبة لِلصّ: إنّه يَهوى تَصميم فَساتين العَرائِس. يَقضي بندق أوقات الفِراغ، وهي قليلة، في مُتابَعة صُوَر الأفراح حول العالَم لِيَدرُس تَفاصيل فَساتين العَرائِس. يدرس الزَخرَفة، وطَريقة القَصّ، ونَوع القُماش، ويُحاوِل أن يعرف كم عَدَد الأمتار المُستَخدَمة في تَفصيل الفُستان. سرّ بندق العجيب هو أنّه، لو لم يكن محاسباً ولصّاً، فإنه كان يحبّ أن يكون مُصَمِّماً لِفساتين الأفراح.

وبالصُّدفة، في نفس اليوم الذي فتح فيه الحساب السرّيّ للقفّاز الأسود، كان بندق يكتب ايميل لِمَوقع مجلّة «عروس تلّ العسل» لِيَسأل الخالة نرجس بعض الأَسئِلة عن فُستان رائِع في صَفحة ستّة وستّين من العَدَد الأسبوعيّ يوم الخميس الماضي.

هناك ناحية أخرى لشخصيّة بندق العجيب

Chapter 6 Language and Culture Notes

- زَعيم = leader, boss
- أشعُر بـالفَخر والسَّعـادة = I feel pride and happiness
- ضَربة قَوِيّة كالزِلزال = an intensive earth-moving strike ("a strong blow like an earthquake")
- أيّـهـا البَرغوث الأبلَه = you stupid flea; later Bunduq is called an ant (نَملة), a cockroach (صِرصـار), and a mosquito (بـاعوضـة)
- اِنكَمَشَت الاِبتِسامة = the smile shrunk
- لَم يُكَمِّل جُملَتـه = didn't finish his sentence
- اِتَّسَع = widened; the root is وسع but the و drops out in this form (VIII)
- بَريق = spark/shine
- عُنُق = neck
- خَراب = ruins; here used to mean "ruinous"
- اِستَعِدّ للمَوت = prepare to die ("for death")

الفَصل السادس

اِبتَسَمَ بندق العجيب وقال للقفّاز الأسود، «يا زعيم، أنا أشعُر بالفَخر والسَّعادة اليوم. أرى على الكمبيوتر أنّك تَستَخدِم كلّ يوم الحساب السرّيّ الذي فَتَحتُه لك في بنك النجاح الدوليّ. مليون دينار كلّ يوم يا زعيم! لا بدّ أنّك تُجَهِّز لِضَربة قَويّة كالزِّلزال في منطقة تلّ العسل.» نظر القفّاز الأسود لبندق بِدَهشة. «عَسَل؟ بَصَل؟ ماذا تقول أيّها البرَغوث الأَبلَه؟ أنا لم أَلمِس هذا الحساب!»

اِنكَمَشَت الاِبتِسامة قليلاً من على وجه بندق، «لم تَلمِسه؟ ولكن يا زعيم أنت تَسحَب مليون دينار كلّ يوم من هذا الحساب الذي فَتَحتُه لك من حَوالي ثلاثة شُهور في بنك النجاح الدوليّ. أَظُنّ...أَعتَقِد... أنّك تُجَهِّز... زلزال... أنا...» ولكن بندق لم يُكَمِّل جُملَته لأنّه رأى على وجه القفّاز بعض العَلامات السَيِّئة. اِتَّسَعَت عَيناه لِتُغَطّي نصف وجهه تقريباً واِختَفَى مِنهُما بَريق الحَياة. في لَحظة كانت يَدا القفّاز حول عُنُق بندق المِسكين، وقال، «ماذا تقول يا محاسب الخَراب! هل هناك مَن يَسرِق منّي أنا؟ أنا القفّاز الأسود! أنا أكبر لصّ في العالم! وأنت يا نَملة تقول أن هناك مَن يَسرِق منّي مليون دينار كلّ يوم منذ ثلاثة شهور؟ تسعون مليون دينار؟! اِستَعِدّ للمَوت كالصِرصار!»

- نَظرة ذُعر حَقيقيّ = a look of real terror
- أُسكُت! = Be quiet!
- أعثُر علَيه = I find him
- وَصِيّتك ورِسالة وَداع = your will and a farewell letter
- عَجين = dough, paste; The Black Glove has changed the final letter of عَجيب (extraordinary), threatening to turn "Bunduq the Extraordinary" into "Bunduq the Dough"
- اِنكَب = hunched
- مُخّه يَرتَعِش داخِل جُمجُمته = his brain trembling inside his skull
- تَتَراقَص = dancing around, jumping around; the basic verb يَرقُص simply means dancing, whereas this form (VI) carries the meaning of dancing or jumping around randomly, as lights and shapes might do when the eyes are closed

في لحظة كانت يدا القفاز حول عنق بندق المسكين

الآن، اِختَفَت الاِبتسامة تماماً من على وجه بندق، وحلَّت مَكانها نَظرة ذُعر حَقيقيّ. حاوَلَ بندق أن يردّ، «ولكن يا زعيم...»

«اُسكُت يا باعوضة! أمامك ثلاث دَقائِق فقط لِتَعرَف ثلاثة أشياء. واحد، من هو هذا الذي يسرق منّي؟ اثنان، أين أَعثُر عليه؟ وثلاثة، كيف حَدَثَ هذا؟ وبعد أن تُعطيني الإجابات الثلاثة، سَأُعطيك دَقيقة رابِعة لِتكتُب وَصيّتك ورِسالة وَداع لِوالدتك، ثمّ تَستَعِدّ للمَوت لأنّك سَتُصبِح بندق العَجين وليس بندق العجيب.»

اِنكَبَّ بندق على الكمبيوتر وهو يشعر أن مُخّه يَرتَعِش داخِل جُمجُمَته وأن الحُروف تَتَراقَص أمامه على لَوحة المَفاتيح.

- أحدَث سَحب = the most recent withdrawal
- باهِت = wan, thin, pale
- سَندَوِتش فَلافِل ساخِن = a hot falafel sandwich
- أن تَصرُخ = to scream
- مَحشو = stuffed
- السَلَطة الخَضراء والطَّحينة والحُمُّص = green salad, tahini, and chickpeas; three additional ingredients in a traditional falafel sandwich
- تَمَهَّل يا زَعيم = take it easy, boss
- يَزوم = snarling
- أطلَقَت صَرخة مُدَوّية رَجَّت = she let out an echoing scream that rattled
- كَيف تَجرُؤان على... = how dare you [both]...
- قَبضة حَديديّة = an iron fist
- الهَرج والمَرج = chaos, pandemonium; both these words mean "disorder," and they are often combined for effect
- عَويل = wailing; زَئير = roaring; أنين = groaning

حـاوَلَ بـنـدق أن يُـرَكِّـز في المَهِـمّـة الـتـي أمـامـه. وبعد دقـائق مَرَّت عليه وكأنّها سَنَوات، صـاح، «وجدتُه يـا زعيم! وجدتُه! أَوّلاً، هذا هو أحدَث سَحب تَمَّ صباح اليوم لحساب شَخص اسمه قاسم بابا، وثانِياً، هذا هو عُنوانه في بَلَد اسمها تلّ العسل.»

أمّا عن السُّؤال الثالِث، وهو كيف حدث هذا الخَطأ، فإن بندق لم يَرُدّ، ووَقَفَ بابتسامة باهِتة في وسط الغرفة على أَمل أن يَنسَى القفّاز هذا السؤال بمُرور الوقت.

فَتَحَت بطاطا البـاب وهـي تـأكُل سَندَوِتش فلافِل ساخِن. وحين شَعَرَت بِيَدَين قَوِيتَين حول عُنُقها أرادت أن تَصرُخ، ولكن فَمـهـا كـان مَحشواً بـالفَلافِل والسَلَطة الخَضراء والطَّحينة والحُمُّص. قال بندق، «تَمَهَّل يا زعيم! ليسَت هذه الفَتاة هي قاسم. إن قـاسم هـو اسم رَجُل، وهذه فتاة.» فَكَّرَ القفّاز لَحظة فـيمـا قـالَـه بـنـدق، ثمّ تَرَكَ عُنُق بطـاطـا وهـو يَزوم. اِبتَلَعَت بطاطا ما في فَمها ثمّ أَطلَقَت صَرخة مُدَوّية رَجَّت الشَّبابيك والأبواب. خـرج أبـوهـا من غرفته وصاح، «من أنتُما؟ كيف تَجرُؤَان على...» ولكن قاسم لم يُكمّل جُملته لأنّه شَعَرَ بِقَبضة حَديديّـة تَـهبُط على أَنفه. وبعدهـا بدأ الـهَرج والمَرج. صَراخ بـطـاطـا، وعَويل أمّ بـطـاطـا، وصِيـاح بـنـدق، وزَئير القـفّـاز وأنين قـاسم.

- كُرة الشاطِئ التي هَجَرَها أصحابها = a beach ball whose owners had abandoned it; صاحِب (plural = أصحاب) is a flexible word that can mean "owner," "master," "friend," or "one who has" (followed by an attribute)
- كُتلة شِبه مُستَديرة = an almost round lump
- مُنتَفِخة = inflated
- بَعض دَرَجات البَنَفسَجيّ = several degrees of purple
- مُتَوَسِّلاً = pleadingly
- اِرحَمني = have mercy on me
- بَريء = innocent
- ضَحِية = victim
- سَأَدُلّك علَيه = I will lead you to him
- نَعيم = luxury

ويعد فَترة، كان قاسم يَبدو مثل كُرة الشاطِئ التي هَجَرَها أصحابها في نِهاية الصَّيف الماضي: كُتلة شِبه مُستَديرة على الأرض في رُكن من الغرفة، مُنتَفِخة قَليلا وتُغَطّيها الألوان، أزرق، ووردِيّ، وأحمر، وأسود، ويعض دَرَجات البَنَفسَجيّ. قال قاسم مُتَوَسِّلاً، «أرجوك! اِرحَمني! أنا بَريء! أنا ضَحِية! أنا أخذتُ مليون دينار صباح اليوم. مليون واحد فقط، وليس تسعين كما تقول. أنا أعرف مَن أخذ ملايينك وسَأَدُلّك عليه. سَآخذك إلى قَصره الآن وسَترى النَّعيم الذي يعيش فيه منذ ثلاثة شهور بِأموالك. سآخذك إليه فَوراً واِفعَل به ما تَشاء... آه يا عيني!»

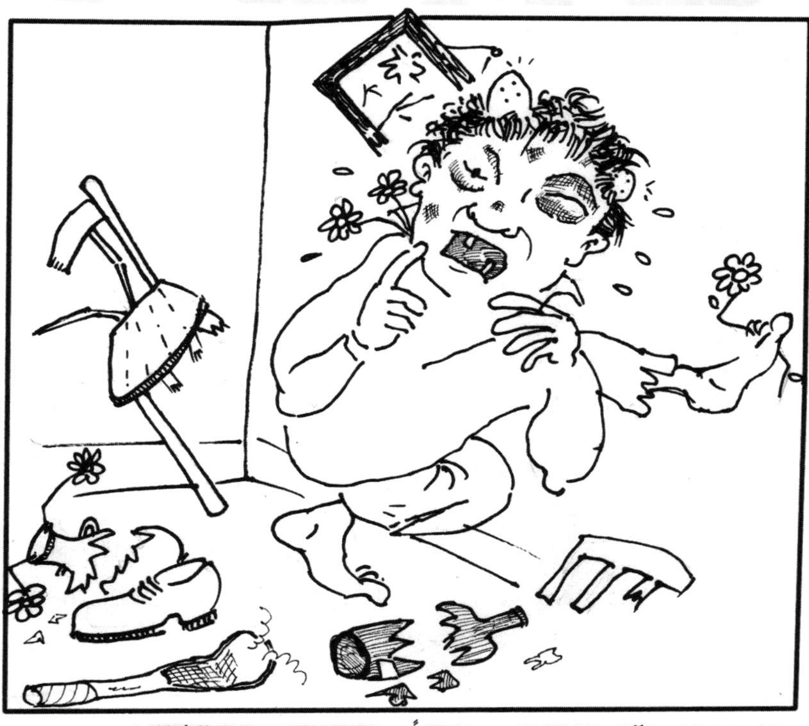

«سآخذك إليه فوراً وافعل به ما تشاء!»

- في الظَّلام = in the dark
- عِند أطراف المدينة = on the outskirts ("on the edges") of the town

Chapter 6 Test your understanding.

1 What did Bunduq think that The Black Glove is planning in Honey Hill?
2 Why did The Black Glove react with horror and anger when Bunduq told him about the withdrawals from the secret bank account?
3 What were the three things he orders Bunduq to find out immediately?
4 What happened to Qasim's daughter, Batata, when she opens the door?
5 Why did Qasim point the finger at Ali Baba?
6 How many trucks were in the convoy?
7 Where was the convoy heading?

وبعد ساعات قليلة، في سُكون اللّيل، تَحَرَّكَت قافِلة من خمس شاحِنات لِتَعبُر تلّ العسل في الظَّلام في طريقها إلى قصر علي بابا عند أطراف المدينة.

في سكون الليل، تحرّكت قافلة من خمس شاحنات

Chapter 7 Language and Culture Notes

- آسِف لإزعاجك = sorry to bother you
- تائِه = lost
- أجهِزة الخَرائِط = navigation systems ("systems for maps")
- يجِب أن تَبيت = you must spend the night; يَبيت is a verb derived from بيت (house) with the meaning of "to stay the night [in the house]"

الفَصل السابع

«أنـا آسِـف يـا سـيـدي عـلـى إزعـاجك في هـذه الساعـة المُتـأخِّـرة، ولكنّـني غريب في هـذا البلد. أنـا تـائِـه، وأجـهِـزة الخَرائِط في شاجِناتي لا تعمل، والشَوارِع خالِية كما ترى، ولا أعرف مَن أسأل عن الطريق. ولكن حين رأيتُ قصرك الجميل قلتُ لنفسي، إن صاحِب هذا القصر الجميل لا بدّ أن يكون رَجُلا كَريماً.»

اِبتَسَمَ علي بابا لمرجانة الواقفة بِجواره عند باب القصر، ثمّ قال للغريب، «أهلاً بك يا أخي، ومَرحَباً. أرجوك، تفضّل بالدُخول. البيت بيتك. يَجِب أن تَبيت هنا الليلة، وفي الصباح، سأدُلّك على طريقك. إلى أين ستذهب غداً إن شاء الله؟»

«البيت بيتك»

- لأحضُر مؤتَمَراً = to attend a conference
- كُبـار المزارِعين = the leading farmers
- مَصانِع الصَّلصة = [tomato] paste factories
- في مَجال = in the area of
- اِختَرَع = invented, made up
- أن يُحرِج ضَيفه = to embarass his guest
- حُسن اِستِقبالك = the warmth of your reception
- بَرميل = barrel (plural = بَراميل)
- حَصاد سَنة كامِلة = a whole year's harvest
- جُهد = effort
- عُقود = contracts (singular = عَقد)
- أمانة في عُنُقي = "a keepsafe in my neck"; an expression meaning that you will guard something with your life
- مَسئُوليّة = responsibility
- أشعُر بالخَجَل = I feel ashamed/embarrassed

رَدَّ القفّاز الأسود، «في الحقيقة يا سيدي أنا تاجِر طماطم، وفي طريقي إلى مدينة «رأس الفيل» لأحضُر هناك مُؤتَمَراً كبيراً جدّاً سَيَحضُره كُبار المُزارِعين، وتُجّار الطماطم، وأصحاب مصانِع الصَّلصة والكَتشَب والعَصير من كلّ البِلاد المُجاوِرة. إنّه أهَمّ مُؤتَمَر لكلّ مَن يعمل في مَجال الطماطم. أكيد أنت سَمِعتَ عَنه، ألَيس كذلك؟»

في الحقيقة علي بابا لم يَسمَع في حَياته عن هذا المؤتمر، ولم يسمع أيضاً عن البلد، وذلك لِسَبَب بَسيط، وهو أن القفّاز الأسود اِختَرَعَ هذه القِصّة. لكن علي بابا لا يُريد أن يُحرِج ضَيفه فقال، «أكيد، أكيد، أسمع عن هذا المؤتمر منذ سنوات. إنه مشهور جدّاً. إنّه أكبر سوق تِجاريّ في مدينة «سِنّ الفيل» والمُدُن المُجاوِرة. أليس كذلك يا مرجانة؟»

«نعم يا سيدي.»

«في الحقيقة يا أخي أنا أشكُرك على كَرَمك وحُسن اِستِقبالك لي، وسَيُشَرِّفني أن أبيت في قصرك الليلة. ولكن، أنا معي في هذه الشاحنات أربعون بَرميلاً. هذه البراميل مَليئة بالطماطم التي سَأعرِضها في المؤتمر. إنها حِصاد سَنة كامِلة من جُهد وعَرَق المُزارِعين البُسَطاء على أمل أن يَحصُلوا على عُقود من مَصنَع صَلصة أو عصير. إنّها أمانة في عُنُقي، ومَسئُوليّة كبيرة. أنا أشعُر بالخَجَل منك يا سيدي.»

قال علي بابا، «لماذا تشعُر بالخَجَل؟ أنا لا أفهم. ما هي المُشكِلة بالضَّبط؟»

- تَفسُد = go bad, go off

- ضَيف ثَقيل = "a heavy guest"; an expression meaning a troublesome or overdemanding guest

- قاعة حَفَلات كَبيرة مُكَيَّفة = a large air-conditioned banquet hall/function room

- أحِبّائي وأصدِقائي = my loved ones and friends; أحِبّاء is the plural of حَبيب; أصدِقاء is the plural of صَديق

- وَهَبت عُمري كلّه لعَمَل الخَير = I have dedicated my entire life to charity (doing good deeds)

- الفُقَراء = the poor; فَقير = poor [person] (plural = فُقَراء)

- ما أروَع هذا الاسم = how wonderful that name is!

- نَبيل = noble

«أخاف أن تَفسُد الطماطم لو تَركناها داخل الشاحنات حتـى الصبـاح بسبب الحرارة. أنـا لا أُريد أن أكـون ضَـيفـاً ثَقيلاً... ولكن هل يُمكِن أن تَبيت البَراميل داخل القصر؟»

ضَحِكَ علي بـابـا وقـال، «أكيد، أكيد. هذا أمر بَسيط جدّاً. اِسمَع، أنا عندي في القصر قاعة حَفَلات كبيرة مُكَيَّفة. سَأُنادي الآن على بعض العُمّال، وسيأخذون بَراميلك إلى القاعة لِتَبيت في التكييف يا سيّد... يا سيّد... قُل لي يا أخي، ما اسمك؟»

«أحِبّائي وأصدِقائي، مثلك أنت يا سيدي، يُسَمّونني القفّاز الأبيض لأنّني وَهَبتُ عُمري كلّه لِعَمَل الخَير ومُساعَدة الفُقَراء.»

قـال علـي بـابـا، «يـا سـلام! مـا أروَع هـذا الاسـم. القـفّـاز الأبيض! كَم أنتَ نَبيل يا سيّد قفّاز! فِعلاً، ليس هنـاك أفضَل من عَمَل الخَير ومُساعَدة الفُقَراء. أليس كذلك يا مرجانة؟»

«نعم يا سيدي.»

«كَم أنتَ نبيل يا سيّد قفّاز!»

مُتعَب وجَوعان = tired and hungry

أروَع وأشهَى وألَذّ = the most wonderful, most delicious, and tastiest

تَفَضَّل لِتَستَريح = come in and rest

Chapter 7 **Test your understanding.**

1 What excuse did the visitor give for knocking at Ali Baba's door?
2 Where did he say he is heading? What does the name of the town mean literally?
3 What kind of conference did the visitor say he is attending there?
4 Why did Ali Baba pretend to have heard of the destination and the conference?
5 What did the visitor say is in the trucks?
6 Why did he say he is worried about leaving his cargo in the trucks?
7 What did Ali Baba offer the visitor and his cargo?
8 What was Murjana going to prepare for the guest and Ali Baba?

«تفضّل بالدُخول يا سيّد قفّاز. أنا سَعيد بزِيارتك. لا بدّ أنك مُتعَب وجَوعان. هَيّا بِنا نأكل شيئاً خَفيفاً معاً. مرجانة تُعِدّ أروَع وأشهَى وألَذّ بيتزا في كلّ تلّ العسل والمدن المجاورة. أليس كذلك يا مرجانة؟»

«نعم يا سيدي.»

«مرجانة سَتُعِدّ لنا طَبَقَين من البيتزا الشَهيّة. تفضّل لِتَستَريح بالداخِل. غداً أمامك سَفَر طَويل قبل أن تَصِل إلى مؤتمرك في مدينة أُذُن الفيل.»

Chapter 8 Language and Culture Notes

- حِوار مع نَفسها = a dialogue with herself
- قَلَق = concern, worry
- بِالتَّحديد = precisely
- الجُبن المَبشور = grated cheese
- لم أسمَعه يَذكُر = I didn't hear him mention
- أعواد الرَّيحان = sprigs of basil
- ذَيل = tail
- أيّ جُزء آخَر = any other part
- أدراج = drawers (singular = دُرج)
- مِرقاق = rolling pin
- تَعَطَّلَت = broke down
- فَلطَحة العَجين = flattening the dough
- غُرَباء = strangers (singular = غَريب)

الفَصل الثامن

دَخَلَت مرجانة المَطبَخ لِتُعِدّ البيتزا. بدأَت حِواراً مع نفسها، «أنا أشعر بالقَلَق.» وفتحَت باب الثَّلاّجة.

«ولكنني لا أعرف لماذا بالتَّحديد.» ثمّ أخذَت كُرَتَين من العَجين.

«بل تعرفين تماماً يا مرجانة! إنّه هذا الضَّيف الغَريب.» ثم أَخرَجَت عُلبة من الجُبن المَبشور.

«أبي أكبر تاجر خُضار في تلّ العسل ولم أسمَعه يَذكُر بلداً اسمها رأس الفيل أبداً.» ثمّ قَصَّت بعض أعواد الرَيحان.

«ولا ذَيل الفيل ولا أيّ جُزء آخَر من جِسم الفيل، أو أيّ حَيَوان آخَر.» ثمّ فتحَت أحد الأدراج.

«ولم أسمع من أبي أن الطماطم لها مؤتمرات!» وأخرجَت المِرقاق.

«أجهِزة الخَرائِط تَعَطَّلَت في خمس شاحِنات في نفس الوقت؟ صُدفة غريبة!» ثمّ أحضَرَت زُجاجة من زَيت الزَّيتون.

«وأيضا، هذا الرجل اسمه غريب. القفّاز الأبيض؟ يبدو لي أنّني سمعتُ هذا الاسم من قبل، ولكن أين سمعتُه؟ متى سمعتُه؟» ثمّ بدأَت في فَلطَحة العَجين.

«أنا أعرف أن الناس الذين يَهِبون حَياتهم لعَمَل الخَير ومُساعَدة الفُقَراء لا يحبّون أن يَذكُروا ذلك أمام الغُرَباء.» ثمّ ذهبَت لإحضار بعض الطماطم. ولكن... أين الطماطم؟

- حَبّة = "one [tomato] fruit"; حَبّة (plural = حَبّات) is a word that can be used for a single unit of many items in the natural world, for example grain, seed, kernel, berry, etc.

- لَن تَنفَع = will not work ("be usable")

- طازَج = fresh

- لَن يَشعُر بالفَرق = will not feel the difference

- لِتُحاوِل أن تَتَذَكَّر = to try and remember

- مِفتاح النور الرَّئيسيّ = the main light switch; مِفتاح can mean "key" or "switch"

- لم تُستَخدَم = it hadn't been used; an example of the passive, formed by changing the vowel pattern of the verb: يَستَخدِم = use (active), يُستَخدَم = be used (passive)

- مُناسَبات رَسميّة = official occasions

«لم أسمع أن الطماطم لها مؤتمرات!»

بَحَثَت مرجانة في كلّ مكان ولكنّها لم تَعثُر على حَبّة طماطم واحدة. لَن تَنفَع البيتزا دون الطماطم. ما العمل؟ وجاءَتها فِكرة. إن في قاعة الحَفَلات الكبيرة أربعون برميلا من الطماطم الطازَجة الفاخِرة، لو أخَذَت حَبّتَين أو ثلاث حَبّات فلَن يشعر السيّد قفّاز بالفَرق.

دخلَت مرجانة قاعة الحفلات الكبيرة ووقفَت لَحظة لِتُحاوِل أن تَتَذَكَّر أين مِفتاح النور الرَئيسيّ لهذه القاعة الشاسِعة. مرجانة لا تأتي إلى هذه القاعة كَثيراً لأنّها لم تُستَخدَم في مُناسَبات رَسميّة من قبل. وبَينما هي تُفكِّر،

- صُفوف = rows, lines (singular = صَفّ); also used for a grade in school: الصَّفّ الثالِث = the third grade
- مَرصوص = lined up, arranged in rows
- تَخَيَّلَت = she imagined
- عَطسة = a sneeze; يَعطِس = sneezes
- تَسَمَّرَت مرجانة في مكانها = Murjana was nailed to the spot; the verb is from the same root as مِسمار (a nail)
- تَوَقَّفَت عن التَنَفُّس = she stopped breathing
- بالغَريزة = by instinct, instinctively
- بحِرص شَديد = with extreme caution
- غِطاء = lid, cover
- كادَ قلبها يَتَوَقَّف = her heart nearly stopped
- The gang members have various *noms de guerre*: خَنجَر الصَّباح (Dagger of the Morning); جَزّار الصَّحراء (Butcher of the Desert); أنياب اللَّيل (Fangs of the Night); أنهار الدَّم (Rivers of Blood)

كانت تَنظرُ إلى صُفوف البَراميل المَرصوصة على اليمين وعلى اليسار، لِتَختار منها برميلا تأخذ منه حبّات الطماطم. وفَجأةً، تَخيَّلَت أنّها سمعَت عَطسة. برميل يَعطِس؟ تَسمَّرَت مرجانة في مكانها وتَوَقَّفَت عن التَّنَفُّس. مرجانة تشعر بالغَريزة أن هناك خَطَر.

اِقتَربَت مرجانة من برميل على يمينها بحِرص شَديد، ووَضَعَت أُذُنها على الغِطاء. وفجأةً، كادَ قَلبها يَتَوَقَّف حين سمعَت صوتاً يأتي من برميل على يسارها وهو يقول، «يا خَنجَرَ الصَّباح، هل سمعتَ شيئاً؟».

سمعت صوتاً يأتي من برميل

- إشارة (الهُجوم) = signal, sign (of attack)
- ثَقيل السَّمع = hard ("heavy") of hearing
- قَد يَسمَعنا أحَد الخَدَم = one of the servants might hear us
- على حَقّ = correct, right
- أُصيبت مرجانة بحالة من الذُّعر = Murjana was struck by a state of terror
- كُتلة من الثَّلج = a block of ice
- شَجاعة = courage
- اِنهِيار = breaking down, collapsing
- بِبُطء شَديد = very slowly
- أطلَقَت ساقَيها إلى الريح = she ran like the wind ("freed her legs to the wind")

Chapter 8 Test your understanding.

1 Why was Murjana suspicious of the guest?
2 Why did she go to the banquet hall?
3 What was the first thing she heard while searching for the light switch?
4 Which of the thieves was hard of hearing?
5 Why does one of the thieves tell the others to be quiet?
6 How does Murjana leave the room?

ردّ عليـه صَوت آخَر من برميل مُختَلِف، «لا يـا جَزّار الصَحراء لم أسمع شيئاً بعد. وأنت يا أنياب الليل، هل سمعتَ الإشارة؟» ردّ عليه صوت آخر من برميل أَبعَد قليلاً، «لا، لم أسمع الإشارة بعد. ولكن أنا كما تعرفون، ثَقيل السَّمع.» وجاء صوت آخر، «يا رِجال! أسكتوا! إن لم تَسكُتوا قَد يَسمَعنا أحد الخَدَم فَيَنكَشِف أَمرنا.» وجاء صوت آخر، «نعم! أنهار الدَّم على حَقّ. يَجِب أن تَسكُتوا لِنَسمَع إشارة الهُجوم حين تأتينا من القفّاز الأسود. أُسكُتوا!»

أُصيبَت مرجانة بِحالة من الذُّعر وشعرَت وكأنّها تحوَّلَت إلى كُتلة من الثَّلج. قالت لنفسها، «الشَّجاعة يا مرجانة! هذا ليس وقت الاِنهيار، بل هو وقت التَّفكير السَّريع.» ثمّ عادَت بِخَطَواتها إلى الخَلف باِتِّجاه باب قاعة الحفلات الكبيرة، وخرجَت بِبُطء شَديد، وأَغلَقَت الباب وَراءها، ثمّ أطلَقَت ساقَيها إلى الريح باِتِّجاه المَطبَخ، بدون الطماطم.

Chapter 9 Language and Culture Notes

- أسرَعَت = hurried
- رَوَت له = told him, related to him
- تَلهَث و تَتَلَعثَم = panting and stuttering
- اِبقي داخِل المَطبَخ = stay inside the kitchen! (talking to a female)
- أجرَى مُكالَمة سَريعة = made a quick call
- رِفاقه = his friends, his mates; رِفاق = friends/mates (singular = رَفيق)
- بسُرعة البَرق = as fast as lightening
- مُحاصَر = surrounded
- العِصيّ وسكاكين المَوز = sticks and banana knives
- وَقع أقدام = footsteps
- فوجِئَ = was surprised
- يَركُل = kicking
- يَتَدَفَّقون = bursting in

الفَصل التاسع

أَسرَعَت مرجانة إلى هاتِفها المحمول وطلبَت أبيها ورَوَت له ما حدث وهي تَلهَث وتَتَلَعثَم. قال الأب، «اِطمَئِنّي يا ابنتي. اِبقي داخل المَطبَخ وأَغلِقي الباب على نفسك بالمِفتاح. أنا سأكون معك بعد ثلاث دقائِق. لا تخافي.»

أجرَى الأب مُكالَمة سَريعة إلى قِسم الشُّرطة، ومُكالَمة أسرَع إلى أحد رِفاقه في سوق الخضار. ثمّ جرَى إلى سيّارته واِنطَلَقَ بِسُرعة البَرق نحو قصر علي بابا.

وبعد دقائق كان القصر مُحاصَراً بِرِجال الشُّرطة، وبِعشرات من تُجّار الخضروات والفاكِهة يَحمِلون العِصيّ، وسَكاكين المَوز.

قال علي بابا لِضَيفه، «آه! إنّي أسمَع وَقع أقدام تَقتَرِب. لا بدّ أن تكون البيتزا! سترى بنفسك الآن أن مرجانة تُعِدّ أَلَذّ وأطيَب...» وفجأةً، فوجِئَ علي بابا والقفّاز بِشُرطيّ يَركُل باب حُجرة الجُلوس وبعشرات من رِجال الشرطة وتجّار الفاكهة يَتَدَفَّقون إلى الداخِل.

صاح قائِد الشرطة، «مَن مِنكُما القفّاز الأسود؟»

بِحمولَتها = with their load

مُجرِمون = criminals

مُكَبَّلين بـالسَّلاسِل الحَديديّة = shackled with iron chains

كَم أنـا سَعيد بِلِقـائنـا = how pleased I am that we have met ("with our meeting")

إن طَلَبتَ رَأيي = if you ask my opinion

في حُدود = approximately

سِجن = prison (plural = سُجون); مَسجون = prisoner (plural = مَساجين)

عامّ = public

عَقرَب = scorpion

أشارَ القفّاز إلى علي بابا، وأشارَ على بابا إلى القفّاز، وصاح الاثنان معاً في نفس الوقت،

«هو!»

اِنطَلَقَت شاحنات الشرطة بِحُمولتها من اللُّصوص باتّجاه قِسم شرطة تلّ العسل. أمّا القفّاز الأسود، وبندق العجيب وخَنجَر الصباح، فقَرَّرَ قائِد الشرطة أن يأخذهم معه في سيّارته، فجلس المُجرِمون الثلاثة على المِقعَد الخَلفيّ مُكَبَّلين بالسَّلاسِل الحَديديّة.

وفي الطريق، قال القائد، «يا قفّاز، كم أنا سَعيد بِلِقائنا الليلة! إن طلبتَ رأيي، فأنا أرى أنك ستكون ضَيفنا هنا في تلّ العسل في حُدود ثلاثين أو أربعين عاماً في سِجن تلّ العسل العامّ. المَساجين هناك يُسَمّونه «فُندُق ذَيل العَقرَب». لا أعرف لماذا. ها! ها! ها!»

- حَسَب = according to
- التَّرتيب الأبجَديّ = alphabetical order
- سَيَستَضيفك = will welcome you (as a guest)
- تَسائَلَ = wondered
- ألا تأتي قبل...؟ = doesn't it come before...?
- شَرِكة البَترول = petroleum company
- أربع أيادٍ = four hands

«وبـعـد ذلك سَـتَـتَّـجِـه إلى الـدُّوَل الأُخـرَى الـتـي تُـريـدك أن تكون ضَيفاً في سُجونها. أعتقد أن خَطّ سَيرك من سِجن إلى سِجن سيكون حَسَب التَّرتيب الأبجَديّ لِلدُّوَل التي تريدك. رُبَّما كانت أُستراليا هي أوّل بلد سَيَستَضيفك بعدنا. هـا! هـا! هـا!»

تَسـائَـلَ بندق العجيب وهو يجلس بين القفّاز وخنجر الصباح على المقعد الخلفيّ، «ولكن، ماذا عن أَذربَيجان؟ ألا تأتي قبل أُستراليا في الترتيب الأبجديّ؟ لا بدّ أنّهم يُريدوننا في أذربيجان بسبب مَوضوع سَرِقة شَرِكة البَترول في باكو الذي...» ولكن بندق لم يُكَمِّل جُملته لأنّه شعر بأربع أَيادٍ حول عُنُقه.

«ولكن، ماذا عن أذربيجان؟»

- بَوّابة = gate
- شَرط = condition
- تَتَنازَل (عَن) = renounce, forgo (in favor of)
- أيتام = orphans (singular = يَتيم)
- أرامِل = widows (singular = أرمِلة)

Chapter 9 Test your understanding.

1 What two calls did Murjana's father make when she told him what happened?
2 Who kicked down the door?
3 How long did the police chief say that The Black Glove and his gang are likely to spend in Honey Hill prison?
4 What is the prisoner's nickname for Honey Hill prison?
5 What did the chief say will happen to the gang after that?
6 Why did Bunduq mention Azerbaijan?
7 What question did Ali Baba ask Murjana while they were standing outside his palace watching the thieves being taken away?
8 How did Murjana answer?

وقف علي بابا أمام بَوّابة القصر لِيَنظُر إلى قافلة شاحنات الشرطة وهي تتّجه نحو المدينة، ثمّ قال لمرجانة، «هل تَتَزَوَّجيني يا مرجانة؟»

فَكَّرَت مرجانة قليلاً ثمّ رَدَّت، «نعم. ولكن عندي شَرط واحد. نذهب غداً صباحاً إلى البنك وتَتَنازَل عن كلّ مَلايينك وأملاكك إلى الأيتام، والفُقَراء، والأرامِل، والمُستَشفيات في تلّ العسل. ما رأيك؟»

«عندي شَرط واحد.»

Chapter 10 Language and Culture Notes

- فـي تَمـام التـاسِعة = at exactly nine [o'clock]

- رَفَضـا أن يَتَحَركـا = they [both] refused to move

- كـابوس = nightmare

- تَخَلَّصَ من = he was rid of

الفَصل العاشر

البنك يفتح أبوابه في تَمام التاسِعة، ولكن على بابا ومرجانة كانا أمام الباب على سُلَّم المَدخَل الرئيسيّ الساعة الثامِنة والثُّلث. اِضطرَّ عُمّال النَّظافة الصَّباحيّة أن يُنَظِّفوا سلّم المدخل من حول قَدَمَيهما لأنّهما رَفَضا أن يَتَحَرَّكا من مَكانهما على السلّم.

خرج علي بابا من البنك وهو يشعر أنّه إنسان جديد. أخيراً، اِنتَهَى كابوس القفّاز والبندق والطماطم وخنجر الصباح والبراميل واللُصوص. الآن تَخَلَّصَ من مُكالَمات

رفضا أن يتحرّكا من مكانهما على السلّم

- يَتَزَوَّج حَبيبَته = marry his love
- أن أحتَفِظ = to keep
- فكِّر في سَعادَتهم = think of their happiness
- نَتَبادَل التَهاني = exchange congratulations
- مَبروك! = Well done! Congratulations! (literally "blessed")
- تَلَقَّيتُ وِساماً = I received a decoration/a medal
- تَرقِية إلى مَنصِب كَبير = promotion to a top position
- مَقال = article (in newspaper, etc.)
- على أربَع أعمِدة = over ("on") four columns
- الأرشيف = the archive
- ضِيق الوَقت = lack of time
- تَوكيلات تِجارة المجَوهَرات = jewel trading agencies
- مُكافآت سَخِية = generous rewards
- مَعلومات تُؤَدّي إلى القَبض = information leading to the arrest

قاسم ودَعواته السَّخيفة على الإفطار والغَداء والعَشاء، والشاي والقهوة. الآن يستطيع أن يَتَزَوَّج حَبيبَته ويعيش معها في سَعادة. وقف علي بابا أمام البنك وقال لمرجانة، «أنا اليوم أسعَد إنسان في العالم. ولكنّني كنتُ أودّ أن أحتفِظ بسيّارة ألمانيّة وأُخرَى أمريكيّة، وربّما واحدة إيطاليّة فقط. واليَخت أيضاً كان لا بأس به.»

ضَحِكَت مرجانة وقالت، «ولكن الآن كلّ هذه مِلك الفُقَراء يا حبيبي. فَكِّر في سَعادَتهم.»

فجأةً سمعَت مرجانة صَوتاً يُنادِيها، «يا سيّدة مرجانة! ما أجمَل هذه الصُّدفة أن أجِدك أمام البنك! أنا كنتُ في طريقي إليكم! ها! ها! ها!» إنه قائِد الشرطة الذي قَبَض على العصابة أمس.

«أنا وأنت يجِب أن نَتَبادَل التَهاني يا سيّدة مرجانة! مَبروك لي لأنّني تَلَقَّيتُ وِساماً من المَلِك صباح اليوم، وتَرقِية إلى مَنصِب كبير. هل قَرَأتُما المَقال الذي كَتَبوه عَنّي اليوم في جريدة أخبار تلّ العسل في الصَّفحة السادِسة؟ إنّه على أربعة أعمِدة! للأَسَف اِستَخدَموا صورة قَديمة من الأرشيف بسبب ضيق الوقت! ها! ها! ها! وأنت يا سيّدة مرجانة، مبروك لك لأنّك سَتَحصُلين على ملايين كثيرة جدّاً. هناك عَشرات البُنوك والمَتاحِف وشَرِكات البَترول وتَوكيلات تِجارة المُجوهَرات التي عَرَضَت مُكافآت سَخِية جداً لِمَن يُدلي بِمَعلومات تُؤَدّي إلى القَبض على العصابة!»

- سيِّدة أعمال = businesswoman (businessman = رَجُل أعمال)
- مَتاجِر = stores/trading outlet (singular = مَتجَر)
- تَرعَى = she looks after
- قَناة فضائيّة = satellite (TV) channel
- يُقَدِّم = presenting
- بَرنامَج = program

Chapter 10 Test your understanding.

1 What time were Ali Baba and Murjana waiting at the bank?
2 Why did they go there?
3 Where did they meet the police chief?
4 What rewards did the chief get for his arrest of the gang?
5 Why is he a little upset about his picture in the newspaper?
6 What was being offered for information leading to the arrest of the gang?
7 What work do Murjana and Ali Baba do now?
8 How many children do they have and what are their names?

وهكذا، أَصبَحَت مرجانة سيِّدة أعمال غَنيّة، تُدير شَرِكاتها ومَصانِعها ومَتاجِرها، كما تَرعَى شُؤون أُسرَتها الصغيرة، اِبنها مُرجان واِبنَتها عَليّة. أمّا زَوجها علي بابا فهو يعمل في قَناة تلّ العسل الفِضائية، يُعِدّ ويُقَدِّم بَرنامَج أُسبوعيّ للأطفال اسمه «اِسألوا بابا علي بابا.»

Answers الأجوِبة

 Part 1 الجزء الأوّل

1A

1 22
2 Adnan and Basma
3 a small swimming pool
4 photographs of California landmarks
5 architecture
6 the actor Clint Eastwood

1B

a ٢
b ٣
c ٦
d ٥
e ١
f ٤

2A

1 7 days a week
2 Monday
3 plays tennis or goes fishing with his friends
4 the Mexican chef in the restaurant
5 she helps Adnan in buying the fruit, vegetables, and fish
6 music and learning languages
7 in the summer months
8 his aunt and her children (his cousins)

2B

١ أمّا بسمة فَهي تَتَكَلَّم الفرنسيّة.

٢ أمّا عدنان فَهو يلعب التنس.

٣ أمّا جمال فَهو يُرَحِّب بالنُقود.

٤ أمّا جمال فَهو يساعد أباه في المطعم.

٥ أمّا بسمة فَهي تُدَرِّس اللُغة العربيّة للأطفال.

٦ أمّا عدنان فَهو لا يذهب إلى المطعم يوم الاثنين.

3A

1 in Damascus
2 her mother, Bajiha, and her brother, Fadi
3 they are sisters
4 bags, Fadi's bike, wooden boxes, and an ancient black piano with three legs
5 manager of a dental practice
6 the Syrian dentist in the practice
7 from 5 PM until 10:30 PM, Saturday through Wednesday
8 helps her mother with the housework

3B

١ F
٢ T
٣ T
٤ F
٥ F
٦ F
٧ F
٨ F
٩ T
١٠ T

4A

1 c

2 b

3 a

4 c

5 a

6 b

4B

١ ث

٢ د

٣ ج

٤ ح

٥ ت

٦ ا

٧ ب

٨ خ

5A

1 عَزيزَتي (to a female); عَزيزي (to a male)

2 Thursday afternoon

3 no (via London)

4 two months (July and August)

5 Lebanon, Jordan, and Egypt

6 next year

7 no, because he cannot leave the restaurant for a long period

5B

City	Arrival	Departure
San Francisco		Thursday 5 PM
London	Friday noon	Friday approx 5 PM
Damascus	Saturday approx 3 AM	

6A

1 b

2 c

3 b

4 b

5 a

6 a

Review 1

7A

1 an hour early

2 advertisements for perfume, drinks, car rental companies, and airlines

3 her husband

4 his fiancée, because he was very elegant and was carrying a bouquet of red flowers

5 his manager at work, because he was wearing formal clothes and carrying papers and files

6 yes

7 running and shouting

8 no, because it was as if she was watching scenes from a movie

7B

١ وصلَت زهرة قبل الطائرة بساعة.

٢ في المطار قرأَت زهرة الإعلانات.

٣ جلسَت تتخيّل قِصَص الناس.

٤ كان الشاب يحمل باقة من الزهور الحمراء.

٥ كان الرجل يلبس ملابس رسميّة.

٦ كان الرجل يحمل بعض الأوراق والملفّات.

٧ كان الجوّ حارّاً.

٨ كان الأطفال يجرون ويصيحون.

٩ كان الرجال يُقبّلون أيدي أمّهاتهم.

١٠ مرّ الوقت سريعاً.

8A

1 b

2 c

3 b

4 a

5 a

6 c

8B

١ يَتَحَدَّثون في مَواضيع مُختَلِفة

٢ لِيَنام قَليلاً

٣ نَسمات الفَجر الأولَى

٤ وهي تَبدَأ يَوماً جَديداً

٥ نُسخة من أمّه

٦ كان يَشعُر بالتَعَب

٧ مُنذُ حوالي ٢٥ عاماً

٨ أسَرَت قَلب أختها

9A

1 in the old part of Damascus
2 more than sixty
3 narrow
4 for hundreds of years
5 Souk Al-Hamideyya (Al-Hamideyya market)
6 in Damascus, all the shops in a street sell the same items (e.g., tennis rackets)

9B

Meaning	Singular	Plural
sound	صَوت	أصوات
shape	شَكل	أشكال
color	لَون	ألوان
market	سوق	أسواق
(shop) sign	لافِتة	لافِتات
shop/store	دُكّان	دَكاكين
racket	مِضرَب	مَضارِب
year	سَنة	سِنين

10A

1 two rooms in a 3-star hotel: one double room for Jamal and Fadi, and one single room for herself

2 because there were many families from the Gulf States spending the summer vacation in Lebanon

3 by (shared) taxi

4 "service" taxi

5 two days

6 due to the traffic on the road between Damascus and Beirut, at the border crossing, and in Beirut itself

10B

١ **T**

٢ **F**

٣ **T**

٤ **F**

٥ **F**

٦ **T**

٧ **T**

٨ **F**

11A

1 a man who was a native of Beirut, a Palestinian woman, some young people from the South of Lebanon

2 an Iraqi boy, a girl from the countryside, a young man from the mountains

3 no, he could not hear the differences:

جمال لا يعرف الفَرق في اللَهجة

("Jamal could not tell the difference in the accent")

هو يَرَى أنّهُم جميعاً يتحدّثون اللُّغة العربيّة

("He thinks they are all [just] speaking Arabic")

أنت تَسمَع ما لا أَسمَعه أنا

("You [can] hear what I can't hear")

11B

١ d
٢ h
٣ e
٤ f
٥ c
٦ g
٧ a
٨ b

12A

1 yes, he liked it very much ("a city full of life")
2 girls walking together, some wearing the Hijab and some wearing jeans; fast food restaurants side by side with traditional Lebanese restaurants
3 the sea, mountains, sunshine, blue skies, good fruit, delicious food
4 they always perform their work to the best of their ability
5 the boy making sandwiches in the (spit-roast) restaurant wants his sandwiches to be the tastiest ones in the city

12B

١ بعد أُسبوعَين في بيروت
٢ أَعجَبَتني دمشق كثيراً
٣ مدينة مَليئة بالتَّنَوُّع
٤ مَأكولات أمريكيّة تقليديّة
٥ بلَدهُم كبير الحَجم
٦ الفاكِهة اللَذيذة
٧ أَحسَن شيء
٨ أَهَمّ مدينة
٩ الشابّة التي كانَت تُجَهِّز السَّندَوِتشات
١٠ في مطعم السَّمَك
١١ في رَأينا
١٢ الناس سُعَداء بِهذا النَّجاح

Review 2

							1 d	i	s	h	e	2 s					3 s	
4 b		5 h										6 u	n	i	q	u	e	
e		7 a	i	r	p	l	a	n	e			c					c	
i		p										c		8 y	e	a	r	s
r		p		9 o				10 m	a	r	k	e	t				e	
u		i		p		11 t						s					t	
12 t	e	n	n	i	s	r	a	c	k	e	t	s						
		e		n		a												
		s		i		13 d	a	m	a	s	c	u	s					
		s		o		i												
				n		14 t	h	e	y	l	15 a	u	g	h				
						i					c							
		16 h	e	k	n	o	w	s			c							
						n					e							
			17 i	n	h	a	b	i	t	a	n	t	s					
						l					t							

13A

1 a
2 b
3 a
4 c
5 c
6 a
7 a

14A

1 by train

2 Beirut

3 5:30 AM, because he wanted to have two or three hours of walking in Petra before it became too hot

4 you can read about Petra and the Roman era; you can see pictures of the caves and tombs

5 like a small [insignificant] human standing in front of a giant achievement

14B

١ قَميص وَرديّ

٢ مدينة تاريخيّة

٣ شَوارِع ضَيِّقة

٤ طريق صَحراويّ

٥ كُهوف جميلة

٦ جِبال شاهِقة

٧ مَعلومات واضِحة

٨ تِلال بَعيدة

٩ بيت صغير الحَجم

١٠ آثار رومانيّة

15A

1 b

2 c

3 b

4 a

5 c

6 b

16A

1 it seemed much the same as Aqaba because of the traffic, the noise, and the number of cars competing for space

2 bags/cases, boxes/chests, large plastic bags, cardboard boxes
3 a Japanese fan, a Chinese television, a Korean refrigerator
4 Kuwait, the Emirates, Qatar, Bahrain, Saudi [Arabia]
5 Saudi

16B

١ **f**
٢ **g**
٣ **a**
٤ **e**
٥ **h**
٦ **d**
٧ **c**
٨ **b**

Review 3

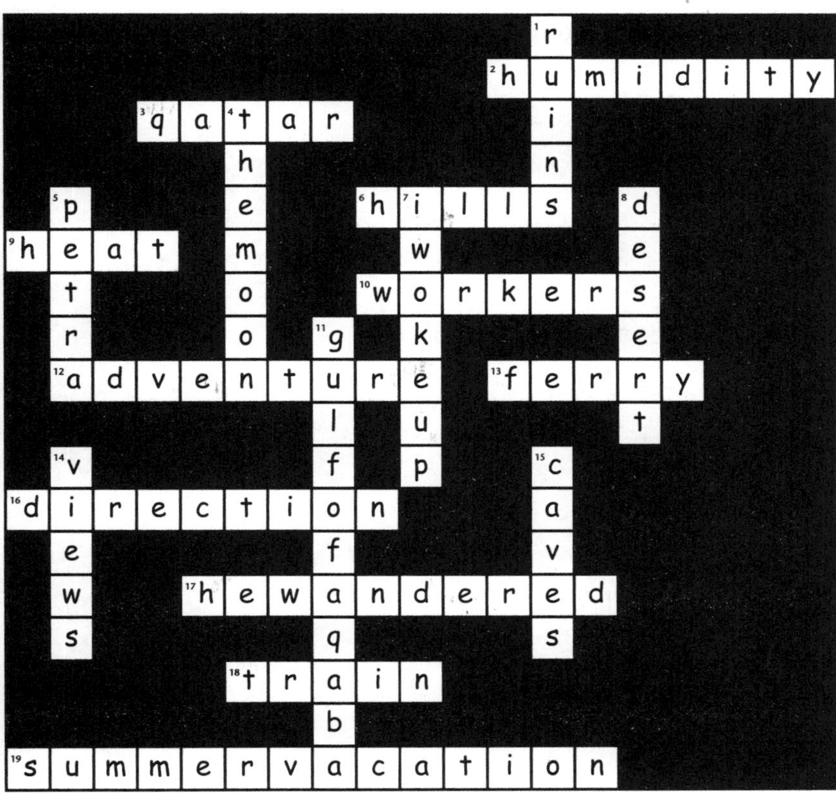

17A

1 Saint Catherine's Monastery (in Sinai)
2 some camels
3 white
4 black
5 two boys from Sweden, another boy from Argentina, and two girls from Scotland
6 about 2 AM
7 the sunrise
8 a lot of young people from around the world who also had the same plan

17B

١ T
٢ F
٣ T
٤ F
٥ F
٦ T
٧ F
٨ T

18A

١ من شرم الشَّيخ
٢ لِزهرة وفادي
٣ لا، قَضَى نصف يوم
٤ عصير فَواكِه لذيذ
٥ غداً
٦ الأهرام
٧ دمشق
٨ لأن رِحلَته اِقتَرَبَت من نِهايَتها

18B

١ شربتُ عَصيراً سوريّاً.

٢ هو خَليط من فواكِه صَيفيّة

٣ غداً سَآخُذ القِطار إلى القاهِرة.

٤ قَضَيتُ يومَين في شَرَم الشَّيخ.

٥ سأعود إلى القاهرة في الصباح.

٦ سأقضي نصف يوم هناك أزور فيه الأَهرام.

٧ زِيارتي اِقتَرَبَت من نِهايَتها للأسف.

٨ كنتُ أودّ أن أشتَري بعض الهَدايا.

19A

1 a

2 c

3 b

4 b

5 c

6 a

19B

١ أنف

٢ صَدر

٣ رَقَبَة

٤ ذِراع

٥ كَتِف

٦ ضُلوع

٧ شَفة

٨ كوع

20A

١ بالتاكسي

٢ حوالي ستّين عاماً

٣ قُبَّعة قُطنيّة ونَظّارة شمس رخيصة

٤ لا، جلس جمال بجانب السائق

٥ رَكِب جَمَلاً وأخذ صُوَراً كثيرة للأهرام وأبو الهول

٦ مَنصور

٧ ٣٠ دولاراً لنفسه و٢٠ دولاراً لمنصور

٨ ٥ دولارات له و دولار واحد لمنصور

٩ قُبَّعة من تكساس

١٠ بعض التُّفاح الأمريكيّ الفاخر

21A

1 Bahija, Zahra, and Fadi
2 tomorrow
3 no, never
4 the way people drive very fast and use the horn a lot
5 the food, the old architecture, the monuments, the weather, the sense of history all around, the people
6 their generosity in spite of of hardship and how they laugh and solve problems between themselves

21B

1 after dinner
2 every minute
3 many things
4 actually

5 the old architecture
6 I didn't feel lonely
7 the thing you liked the most
8 they use the horn(s) a lot
9 despite the difficulties of life
10 as if life [is going to] end tomorrow

22A

1 c
2 a
3 c
4 c
5 b

22B

Recipient	Gift
Julia	silver earrings
Nancy	multicolored hat
Jack	orange T-shirt
George	blue T-shirt
Stephen	green T-shirt
Danny	backgammon set
his parents	Syrian candy/cakes

Review 4

								[1]b						
						[2]f		[3]l	i	p				
	[4]i	[5]c	e			r		o						
		a				[6]i	a	g	r	e	e	d		
	[7]m	i	n	u	t	e								
[8]m		r				n								
o		o				d		[9]m				[10]c		
n						[11]s	u	i	t	a	b	l	e	
a								d				o		
s		[12]h			[13]p			n				t		
[14]t	h	e	p	y	r	a	m	i	d	[15]s		h		
e		b			i			g		w		e		
r		o			c			h		e		s		[16]h
y		u			e			t		d				a
		g			s		[17]n			[18]e	g	y	p	t
		h					o			n				
		[19]t	o	u	r	i	s	t						
							e							

Part 2 الجزء الثاني

1 Ahmed Shawqi

1 "the Prince of Poets"
2 his father was Iraqi, his mother was mixed Turkish and Greek
3 in the royal palace in Cairo because his grandmother worked there
4 a museum containing some of his papers and books
5 in the museum garden in Cairo, and in the park of [Villa] Borghese in Rome
6 to Spain because the political content of some of his poems caused problems with the royal palace and the British government
7 learning Spanish and studying the monuments of the Islamic civilization in Andalusia

2 Haroun Al-Rashid

1 763–809 AD (170–193 AH)
2 poets = شُعَراء; translators = مُتَرجِمين; artists = فَنّانين; linguists = لُغَوِيّين; literary figures = أُدَباء; engineers = مُهَندِسين; scientists/learned men = عُلَماء
3 House of Wisdom (بيت الحِكمة)
4 from central Asia in the east to the Atlantic Ocean in the west
5 outstanding military leader, talented politician
6 tax income increased because of the power of the state

3 Omm Kalthoum

1 in a small village in the Egyptian countryside in 1898
2 he was the village muezzin
3 about six years old
4 she wore boy's clothes
5 the radio and the television
6 a handkerchief
7 elegant, mindful of her appearance, very thick dark hair (as black as the night), small hands and feet, slight build

4 Ibn Battuta

1 in Tangiers in the 14th century AD

2 about twenty years old

3 Algeria, Tunisia, Libya, Egypt, Syria, Saudi Arabia, India, China

4 four-wheel drive vehicles, trucks to carry provisions, airplanes, trains, cellphones, Internet, hotel rooms, restaurants, car and motobike rental

5 the stars at night; the position of the sun in the day

6 camels, donkeys, mules, horses, on foot

5 Mai Ziyada

1 Palestinian, Lebanese and Egyptian

2 she studied Latin, German, Spanish and Italian; she taught English and French

3 through her poetry, writings in literary magazines and newspapers, speeches, lectures, and novels

4 philosophy, Islamic history, and Arabic literature

5 the piano

6 in Cairo

7 on Tuesdays

Part 3 الجزء الثالث

Chapter 1

1 two rooms
2 he walks
3 he is an employee in the editorial department of The Honey Hill Publishing & Distribution House
4 Captain Reesha, Dr. Yaqoot Abul Dhahab, Aunt Narjis
5 a million dinars
6 Al-Najah International Bank
7 584600
8 Open Sesame

Chapter 2

1 to check whether the transfer of a million dinars had gone through to his personal account
2 one million and ninty-nine dinars
3 ninty-nine dinars
4 to go personally to his bank
5 8:20 AM
6 he transfered another million dinars from Al-Najah International Bank and then called the automatic telephone banking service again to check if his personal balance had increased by another million

Chapter 3

1 steam bath from Turkey; sauna from Finland; personal trainer from Sweden; barber from France; piano teacher from Italy
2 the beautiful daughter of a rich neighbor, an important vegetable wholesale trader. She won the title of "Honey Hill Beauty Queen" four years running.

3 because he was poor and he was afraid that Murjana would reject his approaches

4 the International Bank, the United Nations, the White House, Interpol, Scotland Yard

5 half a ton of gold from the Central Bank in South Africa, ten bags of diamonds from a warehouse in Belgium, jewels from one of the ruling families in the Gulf, three Picasso paintings from a steel safe buried under the mansion of a Texas millionaire

6 1, because he doesn't leave finger prints; 2, because his father forced him to work in his leather business and he hated the smell of the leather; 3, because he likes to strangle his enemies with his bare hands, rather than using guns or daggers

Chapter 4

1 to chase late subscriptions

2 Qasim became friendly, always calling him on his cell phone and inviting him around

3 Batata is Qasim's daughter; Umm Batata is her mother (Qasim's wife)

4 to record what he does on his computer

5 it recorded Ali Baba logging onto the website of the Al-Najah International Bank to collect another million dinars

6 they entered the same PIN and password into the website of the Al-Najah International Bank and collected a million dinars

Chapter 5

1 the accountant

2 money laundering, because he thinks it is a superior crime that does not suit ordinary criminals

3 he is interested in wedding dress design

4 *Honey Hill Bride* magazine

5 he was sending an e-mail to the Black Glove about the new secret bank account and accidentally sent the e-mail to "Aunt Nirjis" at the magazine

Chapter 6

1 a major intensive crime spree that required a lot of cash
2 because he didn't know anything about the withdrawals and hadn't taken any money himself
3 1, who is stealing from him; 2, where can he find this person; 3, how did it happen
4 the Black Glove immediately tried to strangle her
5 to save himself
6 five trucks
7 to Ali Baba's mansion

Chapter 7

1 he was lost and the navigation systems in the trucks had broken down
2 to the town of Ra's Al-feel, literally Elephant's Head
3 a conference for tomato farmers, traders, and owners of factories producing tomato paste, ketchup, and juice
4 so as not to embarrass the stranger
5 forty barrels of tomatoes
6 in case they went bad in the heat of the night
7 he offered to let the stranger stay the night and to put the barrels of tomatoes in the large air-conditioned function room
8 pizza

Chapter 8

1 1, because it was unlikely that all the navigation systems would break down at once; 2, because she had never heard of Ra's Al-feel or its tomato conference; 3, because someone who dedicates his life to good works didn't usually boast about it; 4, because the name "The White Glove" sounded familiar

2 because she could not find any tomatoes in the kitchen

3 a sneeze

4 Fangs of the Night

5 because one of the servants might hear them, and so that they could hear the signal to attack

6 she backed out quietly and very slowly, shut the door, then ran as fast as she could

Chapter 9

1 1, to the police; 2, to his friends in the vegetable market

2 a policeman

3 30 or 40 years

4 Scorpion's Tail Hotel

5 they would be passed to the other countries that wanted them

6 because the police chief had speculated that the countries would be in alphabetical order, starting with أُستراليا (Australia), but Bunduq pointed that they were also wanted in أَذَربَيجان (Azerbaijan), which comes earlier in the Arabic alphabet

7 to marry him

8 yes, but on condition that Ali Baba gave away all his money to the orphans, poor, widows, and hospitals in Honey Hill

Chapter 10

1 8:20 AM

2 to give away the money

3 outside the bank

4 a medal from the king and a promotion to a top position

5 because it was an old one from the archive

6 several generous rewards of many millions

7 Murjana became a rich businesswoman, and Ali Baba became a children's presenter on satellite television

8 two: a boy called Murjan, and a girl called Aliya

Glossary الفِهرِست

Note that the Arabic–English Glossary runs in the Arabic direction, i.e., from right to left. It starts on page 223 and runs toward the middle of the book until page 200.

The Arabic–English Glossary contains all the key vocabulary in *Easy Arabic Reader* in Arabic alphabetical order for easy reference. You can look up a word in the Glossary if you need to remind yourself of its meaning.

The Glossary and notes next to the main text should give you most of the vocabulary that you need to understand the passages. However, the Glossary does not contain elementary Arabic words that you should be able to recognize; nor does it include alternative meanings not covered in *Easy Arabic Reader*. For these you will need to use a more comprehensive Arabic–English dictionary such as *A Dictionary of Modern Written Arabic* (Hans Wehr).

Note the following:

- The Arabic words are in strict alphabetical order, rather than in order of their root letters.
- Arabic nouns are followed by their plurals in brackets, if appropriate: e.g.,

  island.............................. جَزيرة (جُزُر)

- Arabic verbs are shown in the past tense followed by the present tense and are indicated in English using the infinitive ("to") form: e.g.,

  to think/believe.............. اِعتَقَدَ/ يَعتَقِد

Islamic lunar calendar .... هِجريّ (هـ)

gift................................. هَدِيّة (هَدايا)

crescent ....هِلال

engineering .... هَندَسة

architecture................هَندَسة المِعمار

hobby ....هِواية (ات)

و

oasis .... واحة (ات)

spacious.................................... واسِع

fast food.................. وَجَبات سَريعة

to direct/angle............... وَجَّهَ/يُوَجِّه

loneliness....................................وَحدة

to want/wish......................... وَدَّ/يَوَدّ

farewell..وَداع

weight .... وَزن (أَوزان)

pillow.........................وِسادة (وَسائِد)

decoration/medal........وِسام (أَوسِمة)

handsomeness...................... وَسامة

means/method.......... وَسيلة (وَسائِل)

will/testament......... وَصيّة (وَصايا)

position...................... وَضع (أَوضاع)

to promise.......................... وَعَدَ/يَعِد

to stand/stop.................. وَقَفَ/يَقِف

state..................................وِلاية (ات)

to dedicate....................... وَهَبَ/يَهِب

and so on............................... وهكَذا

ي

saphhire .... ياقوت

orphan.............................يَتيم (أَيتام)

should/to be necessary that.. يَجِب أن

yacht.............................يَخت (يُخوت)

hand...................................... يَد (أَيدٍ)

nearly...يَكاد

you can.............................. يُمكِنك أن

the day off....................... يَوم العُطلة

Greek................................. يونانيّ

End of Arabic–English Glossary
(The Glossary runs right to left starting on page 223.)

مَوقع (مَواقِع) .... location/website

مَوقِف (مَواقِف) .... situation

مَوهِبة (مَواهِب) .... talent

ميزانيّة (ات) .... budget

ميعاد (مَواعيد) .... time/appointment

ميلاديّ (م) ....
Gregorian "Christian" calendar..........

ميناء (مَوانِئ) .... port/harbor

ن

نائِم (ون/ين) .... asleep

ناحِية (نواحٍ) .... side/aspect

ناسَبَ/يُناسِب ...... to suit/be suitable

ناضِج .... ripe

نَبيل .... noble

نَجاح .... success

نَجم (نُجوم) .... star

نرجسيّ .... narcissistic

نَسَجَ (ينسِج) .... to weave

نُسخة (نُسَخ) .... copy

نَسمة (ات) .... breeze

نَسِيَ/يَنسَى .... to forget

نَشر .... publishing

نِظام (أنظِمة) .... system

نَظرة (ات) .... look

نَعيم .... luxury

نفس الـ... .... the same

نَفسيّ .... psychological

نَفَعَ/يَنفَع .... to work/be usable

نَفي .... exile

نَقَرَ/يَنقُر المَفاتيح .... to type/key

نُقود .... cash

نَملة (نَمل) .... ant

نِهايَة (ات) .... end/completion

نَوَى/يَنوي .... to intend

ه

هاتِف مَحمول (هَواتَف مَحمولة) ....
cell phone/mobile phone..................

هاجَم/يُهاجِم .... to attack

هَبَطَ/يَهبُط .... to fall/go down

هَجَر/يَهجُر .... to abandon/flee

shackled.................................... مُكَبَّل

public library.......... مَكتَبة (ات) عامّة

air-conditioned........................ مُكَيَّف

multicolored............................... مُلَوَّن

navigation .... مِلاحة

مَلعَب (مَلاعِب) ....

playground/playing field/court..........

damned/accursed.................... مَلعون

file .... مِلَفّ (ات)

wrapped................................. مَلفوف

to own.................................. مَلَكَ/يَملِك

beauty queen.................... مَلِكة جَمال

boredom.. مَلَل

full... مَليئ

million......................... مِليون (مَلايين)

enjoyable .... مُمتِع

actor........................... مُمَثِّل (ون/ين)

corridor............................... مَمَرّ (ات)

mixed/blended....................... مَمزوج

beacon/lighthouse .... مَنارة (ات)

suitable.................................... مُناسِب

occasion.......................... مُناسَبة (ات)

midnight..................... مُنتَصَف اللَّيل

inflated.................................... مُنتَفِخ

mine............................ مَنجَم (مَناجِم)

incline/slope .... مُنحدَر (ات)

carved (in stone, etc.)........... مَنحوت

standing/position...................... مَنزِلة

مَنصِب (مَناصِب) ....

position (in a company, etc.).............

area/district............. مِنطَقة (مَناطِق)

skill.................................. مَهارة (ات)

engineer .... مُهَندِس (ون/ين)

hours/opening times.... مَواعيد العَمَل

death.. مَوت

bananas...................................... مَوز

seasonal................................. مَوسميّ

subject/topic........ مَوضوع (مَواضيع)

employee................ مُوَظِّف (ون/ين)

arrival time................. مَوعِد الوُصول

مُسافِر (ون/ين)....traveler/passenger

مُستَدير .... round

مُستَعار .. borrowed/assumed (name)

مُستَورَد .... imported

مُستَيقِظ .... awake

مَسجون (مَساجين) .... prisoner

مَسَحَ/يَمسَح .... to wipe

مُسَدَّس (ات) .... pistol

مَسرَح (مَسارِح) .... theater

مَسرَحيّة (ات) .... play (theatrical)

مَسروق .... stolen

مُشتَرِك (ون/ين) .... subscriber

مَشروع (ات/مَشاريع) .. project/scheme

مُشكِلة (مَشاكِل) .... problem

مَشهَد (مَشاهِد) .... scene

مَشوِيات .... grilled food

مَشي .... walking

مصر للطَيران .... Egypt Air

مَصنَع (مصانِع) .... factory

مَضرَب (مَضارِب) .... racket/bat

مَطار (ات) .... airport

مَطعَم (مَطاعِم) .... restaurant

مَظهَر (مَظاهِر) .... appearance

مُعَدّات .... equipment

مَعرِفة .... knowledge

مَعروضات .... items on display

مَعروف بِـ .... known as/for

مَعالِم .... landmarks

مَعلومات .... information

مُغامَرة (ات) .... adventure

مُفتَرَق الطُّرُق .... crossroads

مُفَكِّر (ون/ين) .... thinker

مُفلِس .... broke/penniless

مَقاس (ات) .... size

مَقال (ات) .... article (newspaper, etc.)

مَقبَرة (مَقابِر) .... tomb

مَقهى (مَقاهٍ) .... café

مُكافَأة (ات) .... reward

مُكالَمة (ات) ....

conversation/call (telephone)...........

مُتَتالٍ .... running/consecutive

مَتجَر (مَتاجِر) .... store/trading outlet

مَتر (أمتار) .... meter

مُتَرجِم (ون/ين) .... translator

مُتعَب .... tired

مُتهالِك .... run-down/shabby

مُتَوَسِّط الحَجم .... medium-sized

مُتَوَسِّل .... pleading/begging

مُتَوَهِّج .... glowing

مَثيل .... (something) comparable

مَجال (ات) .. field/area (e.g., of learning)

مُجاوِر .... neighboring/adjacent

مُجرِم (ون/ين) .... criminal

مُجَوهَرات .... jewels

مُحاصَر .... surrounded

مُحاضرة (ات) .... lecture

مُحَدَّد .... designated/defined

مَحدود .... limited

مَحشُو .... stuffed

مُخّ .... brain

مُخرِج (ون/ين) .... director (movie)

مَخزَن (مَخازِن) ....

storage room/warehouse.................

مَدخَل (مَداخِل) .... entrance

مُدَرِّب (ون/ين) لِلياقة البَدَنيّة ....

physical fitness trainer.......................

مَدرَسة التَمريض .... nursing school

مُدَوَّنة (ات) .... blog/journal

مُدَوٍّ .... echoing

مُدير (مُدَراء) .... manager

مَرَّ/يَمُرّ .... to pass (by)

مُرتاح .... comfortable/at ease

مَرصوص ....

lined up/arranged in rows.................

مِرقاق .... rolling pin

مَرموق .... well-regarded, lofty

مِروَحة (مَراوِح) .... fan

مُزارِع (ون/ين) .... farmer

مَسئُوليّة (ات) .... responsibility

مَسافة (ات) .... distance

لا بَأس بِهِ/بها ....

fairly large/not inconsiderable..........

don’t worry........................ لا تَخَف

I don’t mind........................ لا مانِع

is still/hasn't stopped being... لا يَزال

to notice .... لاحَظَ/يُلاحِظ

sign (above stores, etc.).... لافِتة (ات)

delicious.................................لَذيذ

thief ....لِصّ (لُصوص)

language .... لُغة (لُغات)

mystery/puzzle.................لُغز (ألغاز)

linguist .... لُغَويّ (ون/ين)

meeting............................. لِقاء (ات)

title/nickname ....لَقَب (ألقاب)

Why?... لِمَ؟

to touch....................... لَمَسَ/يَلمِس

to shine.......................... لَمَعَ/يَلمَع

to pant.......................... لَهَثَ/يَلهَث

accent/dialect .... لَهجة (ات)

board (key)...................... لَوحة (ات)

I wish you were................ لَيتك كُنتَ

dishes/foods...................... مَأكولات

conference...................... مُؤتَمَر (ات)

moving/affecting....................... مُؤَثِّر

..............................مُؤَذِّن (ون/ين)

muezzin/caller to prayer...................

historians .... مُؤَرِّخ (ون/ين)

foundation .... مُؤَسَّسة (ات)

writer/author ....مُؤَلِف (ون/ين)

to die............................ ماتَ/يَموت

clever/skillful............................ ماهِر

Well done! Congratulations!..! مَبروك

grated.................................مَبشور

sum (of money)........... مَبلَغ (مَبالِغ)

built.. مَبنٍ

building....................... مَبنَى (مبانٍ)

available............................... مُتاح

remaining/outstanding .... مُتَبَقٍّ

قُبلة (ات)..kiss

قَبيلة (قَبائِل) .... tribe

قَد تَكون .... might be/could be

قَدَم (أَقدام)......................................foot

قَدَّمَ/يُقَدِّم .... to serve/present

قَرَّر/يُقَرِّرَ............................... to decide

قُرط (أقراط)............................ earrings

قَرن (قُرون)............................ century

قَرية (قُرَى) .... village

قِسم (أَقسام)..................... department

قِسم التَّحرير...... editorial department

قِصَّة (قِصَص) .... story

قَصيدة (قَصائِد) .... ode/poem

قَضاء .... spending (time)

قَضى/يَقضي ...... to stay/spend time

قُفّاز (ات).................................. glove

قَلب (قُلوب) .... heart

قَلعة (قِلاع)........................ castle/fort

قَلَق .... concern/worry

قُماش .... cloth

قِمّة (قِمَم)................................ summit

قَناة (قَنَوات)........................... channel

قَناة فَضائيّة .... satellite channel

قِيادة السَّيّارات .... driving

ك

كابوس (كَوابيس) .... nightmare

كامِل .... complete/whole

كَبَس/يَكبِس .... to press/squeeze

كَتِف .... shoulder

كُتلة (كُتَل) .... lump/block

كَثيف .... thick

كَرَّرَ/يُكَرِّر .... to repeat

كَرَم .... generosity

كَسَبَ/يَكسِب .... to earn/gain/win

كُلّما.. whenever

كَلِمة المُرور .... password

كَمَّلَ/يُكَمِّل.......... to finish/complete

كَمّيّة (ات) .... quantity

كَهف (كُهوف) .... cave

كوع.. elbow

pride...فَخر

proud.. فَخور

strawberries.............................. فَراولة

joy/wedding ....فَرَح (أفراح)

to be happy...................... فَرِحَ/يَفرَح

difference....................... فَرق (فُروق)

band (musical)........... فِرقَة موسيقيّة

unique.. فَريد

dress........................ فُستان (فَساتين)

to go bad/go off............. فَسَدَ/يَفسُد

silver (adj.)............................. فِضّيّ

poor .... فَقير (فُقَراء)

idea..................................فِكرة (أفكار)

falafel/chickpea patties........... فَلافِل

Palestine ....فِلَسطين

philosophy ....فَلسَفة

flattening.................................فَلطَحة

art ....فَنّ (فُنون)

artist .... فَنّان (ون/ين)

fruit(s).. فَواكِه

was surprised......................... فوجِئَ

steel.. فولاذ

the early stages of...............في أوائِل

on his mind......................... في ذِهنه

in the care of..................... في رِعاية

elephant...........................فيل (أفيال)

ق

leader .... قائِد (قادة)

to drive...............قادَ/يَقود (السَّيّارة)

reader............................. قارِئ (قُرّاء)

hall...................................... قاعة (ات)

قاعة حَفَلات ....

banquet hall/function room.............

arrivals hall................. قاعة الوُصول

convoys/caravans .... قافِلة (قَوافِل)

to undertake................ قامَ/يَقوم بِـ

law .... قانون (قَوانين)

arrest (of)........................قَبض (على)

fist......................................قَبضة (ات)

hat...................................... قُبَّعة (ات)

عَقرَب (عَقارِب)......................scorpion

عِلاج ....treatment (injury, etc.)

عُلبة (عُلَب) كرتون ......cardboard box

عِلم (علوم) .... knowledge/science

عَلَّمَ/يُعَلِّم ....to teach

على الفَور........................immediately

على حَقّ.........................correct/right

على ما يُرام.............all right, in order

عِملاق (عَمالِقة)..........................giant

عُملة (عُملات) .... currency

عَمَليّة (ات) ......operation/transaction

عَمود (أعمِدة) ....column

عَميق .... profound/deep

عَميل (عُمَلاء) .... client/customer

عُنُق (أَعناق) ....neck

عَنيد.....................................stubborn

عود (أَعواد)...............twig/stick/sprig

عَويل ....wailing

عِيادة (ات)....................clinic/practice

عيد (أَعياد) .... holiday (Eid)

غادَرَ/يُغادِر ....to leave/to depart

غَرَبَ/يَغرُب ....to set (sun)

غُرفة الجُلوس.................sitting room

غُرفة مُزدَوِجة ....double room

غَريب (غُرَباء)........strange/a stranger

غَريزة (غَرائِز)..........................instinct

غَسيل الأموال ....money laundering

غِطاء (أَغطِية).......................lid/cover

غَطّى/يُغَطّي ....to cover

غَنَّى/يُغَنّي ....to sing

فاخِر...................first-class/excellent

فاضَ/يَفيض ....to spill over/flood

فاكِهة (فَواكِه) ....fruit

فَتاة (فَتَيات) ....girl/young woman

فَترة (فَتَرات) .... period (of time)

فَجر .... dawn

فَحم..............................charcoal/coal

ظ

phenomenon .... ظاهِرة (ظَواهِر)

to stay/remain.................... ظَلّ/يَظَلّ

dark...................................ظَلام

ع

family............................... عائِلة (ات)

to live..............................عاشَ/يَعيش

emotion....................(عَواطِف) عاطِفة

scientist/learned person.. عالِم (عُلَماء)

worker/laborer............. عامِل (عُمّال)

to suffer from..........عانَى/يُعاني من

ferry................................ عَبّارة (ات)

Abbasid .... عَبّاسيّ

to cross (over).................. عَبَرَ/يَعبُر

crossing/going across............... عُبور

ancient..عَتيق

to find/come across....عَثَرَ/يَعثُر على

finding............................... عُثور على

extraordinary/remarkable........عَجيب

dough, paste........................... عَجين

عَدَد (أَعداد) ....

issue (of magazine)/number/quantity

enemy.............................. عَدُو (أَعداء)

sweat...عَرَق

bride.......................... عَروس (عَرائِس)

عَزَفَ/يَعزِف على ....

to play (an instrument).....................

dear....................... ...عَزيزي/عَزيزتي

honey.. عَسَل

stick...................................(عِصِيّ) عَصا

gang.............................. عِصابة (ات)

era ....(عُصور) عَصر

perfume.......................... عِطر (عُطور)

to sneeze..................... عَطَسَ/يَعطِس

sneeze...............................(ات) عَطسة

summer vacation......... عُطلة الصَيف

contract.......................... عَقد (عُقود)

to complicate......................عَقَّدَ/يُعَقِّد

complex.......................... عُقدة (عُقَد)

difficulty .... صُعوبة (ات)

line/row...................... صَفّ (صُفوف)

whistle............................ صَفّارة (ات)

blood relation...................... صِلة الدَم

paste/sauce (tomato)........... صَلصة

bald patch.................................صُلعَة

box/chest .... صَندوق (صَناديق)

sound/voice............. صَوت (أصوات)

to photograph............. صَوَّرَ/يُصَوِّر

shouting.................................صِياح

tray......................... صينيّة (صَواني)

ض

slight/tiny .... ضَئيل

lighthearted/amusing........... ضاحِك

to laugh..................... ضَحِكَ/يَضحَك

victim..................... ضَحِية (ضَحايا)

heavily built................... ضَخم الجُثّة

tax .... ضَريبة (ضَرائِب)

rib..............................ضِلع (ضُلوع)

noise/din............................ ضَوضاء

guest.........................ضَيف (ضيوف)

narrow.................................... ضَيِّق

lack of time.....................ضِيق الوَقت

faction .... طَائفة (طَوائِف)

fresh.................................... طازَج

backgammon set.......... طاوِلة الزَّهر

cooking.................................. طَبخ

layer................................ طَبَقة (ات)

drum............................ طَبلة (طُبول)

dentist.......................... طَبيب أَسنان

tahini/sesame paste............... طَحينة

edge...........................طَرف (أَطراف)

the way back................. طَريق العَودة

way/style..................... طَريقة (طُرُق)

child.............................طِفل (أَطفال)

request(ing) .... طَلَب (ات)

throughout...............................طَوال

kindhearted......................طيِّب القَلب

شابّ (شَباب) .... youth/young person

شاحِنة (ات) .... truck

شاسِع .... wide/huge

شاشة (ات) .... screen

شاطِئ (شَواطِئ) .... beach

شاعِر (شُعَراء) .... poet

شّاق .... hard/tiring

شاميّ .... Shami/Syrian

شاهِق .... towering

شاوَرمة .... spit-roast

شَجاعة .... courage

شَجَّعَ/يُشَجِّع .... to encourage

شِدّة .... intensity/strength

شِراء .... buying/purchase

شَرط (شُروط) .. condition/stipulation

شَرِكة (ات) .... company/business

شَعب (شُعوب) .... people/nation

شِعر (أشعار) .... poetry

شقّة (شُقَق) .... apartment

شَكل (أشكال) .... shape

شَهر (شُهور) .... month

شُهرَة .... fame

شَوارِب .... moustache(s)

ص

صاحِب (أصحاب) .... owner

صَبي (صُبيان) .... boy/young man

صِحّيّ .... health(y)

صَحراء .... desert (noun)

صَحراوِيّ .... desert (adj.)

صَدر (صُدور) .... chest

صَدَف .... mother-of-pearl

صَدَّقَ/يُصَدِّق .... to believe

صَديق (أَصدِقاء) .... friend

صِراع (ات) .... struggle

صَرّاف (ون/ين) .... cashier/teller

صَرَخَ/يَصرُخ .... to scream

صَرخة (ات) .... scream

صِرصار (صَراصير) .... cockroach

صَرف .... expenditure

صَعِدَ/يَصعَد .... to rise/go up

ساعَدَ/يُساعِد .... to help

ساكِن (سُكّان) .... inhabitant

ساونا .... sauna

سِجن (سُجون) .... prison

سَحب .... withdrawal

سَحَبَ/يَسحَب .... to withdraw

سَخِي .... generous

سَخيف .... irritating/annoying

سِرّ (أسرار) .... secret

سُرعة (ات) .... speed

سَرَقَ (يسرِق) .... to steal

سَرِقة (ات) .... theft

سِرّيّ .... secret/confidential

سَطح (أَسطُح) .... surface/(flat) roof

سَعادة .... happiness

سِعر (أسعار) .... price

سَعيد (سُعَداء) .... happy

سَقف (أَسقُف) .... ceiling

سَكَتَ/يَسكُت .... to be quiet

سِكّين (سَكاكين) .... knife

سِلاح (أَسلِحة) .... weapon

سِلسِلة (سَلاسِل) .... chain

سَلَطة (ات) .... salad

سُلَّم (سَلالِم) .... steps/stairs

سِمسِم .... sesame

سَميك .... thick

سِنّ مُبَكِّرة .... an early age

سَندَوِتش (ات) .... sandwich

سُهولة .... ease

سوق الجُملة .... wholesale market

سيّارة (ات) أُجرة .... taxicab

سِياسيّ .... political/politician

سيِّدة (ات) أعمال ...... businesswoman

سَيطرة .... control

ش

شُرفة (ات) .... balcony

شَفَة (شِفاه) .... pil

شَمّام .... melon/cantaloupe

شَأن (شُؤون) .... affair/matter

شائِك .... thorny/problematic

formal/official........................ رَسميّ

sip.................................. رَشفة (ات)

balance (bank)...........(أرصِدة) رَصيد

contentment............................ رِضا

humidity.............................. رُطوبة

to graze .... رَعَى/يَرعَى

to look after.................... رَعَى/يَرعَى

to refuse....................... رَفَضَ/يَرفُض

friend/mate.................(رِفاق) رَفيق

neck............................. (رِقاب) رَقَبة

PIN (secret number)...........رقم سرّيّ

digital....................................رَقميّ

to concentrate...................رَكَّزَ/يُرَكِّز

to kick.............................. رَكَلَ/يَركُل

corner............................(أركان) رُكن

novel ....(ات) رِواية

Roman................................. رومانيّ

to tell/to relate................ رَوَى/يَروي

wind.............................. (رِياح) ريح

basil.................................... رَيحان

feather... ريشة

ز

roaring................................زَئير

excessive .... زائِد

to visit............................. زارَ/ يَزور

crowdedness.......................... زِحام

decoration/ornamentation.... زَخرَفة

button................................(أزرار) زِرّ

leader/boss................. (زُعَماء) زَعيم

earthquake..................(زَلازِل) زِلزال

colleague/fellow............(زُمَلاء) زَميل

nominal................................. زَهيد

س

question .... (أسئِلة) سُؤَال

tourist........................ (سُوّاح) سائِح

driver......................... (ون/ين) سائِق

hot.. ساخِن

to walk..............................سارَ/يَسير

bright/shining .... ساطِع

دَرَّسَ/يُدَرِّس .... to teach

دَسَّ/يَدُسّ.................................. to slip

دَقَّ/يَدِقّ............... to knock (on door)

دَقيقة (دَقائِق) .... minute

دُكّان (دكاكين) .... store/shop

دَلَّ/يَدُلّ .... to lead/guide

دَليل سِياحيّ .... tourist guide

دَمعة (دُموع) .... tear

دَهشة .... astonishment

دور (أدوار) .... role

دُوَل الخَليج .... the Gulf states

دَولة (دُوَل) .... state/nation

دَير (أديِرة) .... monastery

دينيّ .... religious

ديوان (دَواوين)..............................

anthology/collection.........................

ذ

ذُعر .... terror

ذَكَرَ/يَذكُر.......................... to mention

ذَكَّرَ/يُذَكِّر.......................... to remind

ذَهَب .... gold

ذَيل (ذُيول) .... tail

ر

رَأى/يَرى .... to see/to think

رَأي (آراء) .... opinion

رُؤية .... visibility

رَئيسيّ.................................. main/chief

رائِع .... fantastic/marvelous

راقَبَ/يُراقِب ...... to observe/to watch

راية (ات) .... banner

رُبَّما .... perhaps

رَجَّ/يَرُجّ .... to shake/rattle

رِجل (أَرجُل).................................. leg

رَجُل (رِجال) أعمال ...... businessman

رَحَّبَ/يُرَحِّب بِـ .... to welcome

رِحلة (ات).............................. journey

رَسا/يَرسو .... to be moored

رِسالة (رَسائِل/رِسالات) ....

letter/message.................................

رَسّام (ون/ين).... illustrators/drawers

swimming pool............ حَمّام سِباحة

chickpeas................................... حُمُّص

load/burden.................. (أحمال) حِمل

load.................................. (ات) حُمولة

dialogue/discussion............(ات) حِوار

approximately.......................... حَوالي

life .... حَياة

خ

servant............................ (خَدَم) خادِم

special/private.......................... خاصّ

aunt (maternal)..................(ات) خالة

shame/embarassment.............. خَجَل

scam/deception ....(خُدَع) خُدعة

exit... خُروج

map .... (خَرائِط) خَريطة

vegetables............................... خُضار

route .... خَطّ السَير

handwriting .... خَطّ اليَد

error............................. (أَخطَاء) خَطَأ

speech .... (خُطَب) خِطاب

danger .... (أخطار) خَطَر

step/stride................ (خَطَوات) خَطوة

airline(s)...................... خُطوط جَوِيّة

fiancée.............................(ات) خَطيبَة

blender............................ (ات) خَلاّط

caliphate................................. خِلافة

mixture....................................... خَليط

caliph .... (خُلَفاء) خَليفة

dagger........................ (خَناجِر) خَنجَر

to strangle.........................خَنَقَ/يَخنُق

charitable .... خَيريّ

thread/cord...................(خُيوط) خَيط

horses.. خَيل

د

income .... دَخل

entry.. دُخول

motorbike .... دَرّاجة (ات) بُخاريّة

drawer...............................(أَدراج) دُرج

degree................................. (ات) دَرَجة

tourist class............... دَّرَجة سِّياحيّة

جَهَنَّمي .... devilish/dastardly

جَوعان .... hungry

جَولة (ات) .... tour

جَيش (جيوش) .... army

ح

حِكمة .... wisdom

حائِط (حَوائِط) .... wall

حاسِب شَخصيّ .... personal computer

حاوَلَ/يُحاوِل .... to try

حَبّ الهال .... cardamom

حَبّة (ات) .... grain, seed, berry, etc.

حَبيب (أَحِبّاء) .... loved one

حَتَّى .... until

حَج .... pilgrimage/hajj

حَجم (أحجام) .... size

حُجوزات .... reservations

حُدود .... border (of country, etc.)

حَديديّ .... iron (made of)

حَديقة (حَدائِق) .... garden

حَديقة حَيَوانات .... zoo

حَذَّرَ/يُحَذِّر .... to warn

حَرب (حُروب) .... war

حِرص .... caution

حِرفة يَدَوِيّة .... handicraft

حَرير .... silk

حَريص .... mindful

حُزن (أحزان) .... sorrow

حِساب (ات) .... account (bank)

حَسَب... .... in accordance with

حِصاد .... harvest

حَضَرَ/يَحضُر .... to attend

حِضن (أحضان) .... hug

حَفر .... digging

حِفظ .. learning by heart/memorizing

حَفلة (ات) .... concert/party

حَلَّ/يَحِلّ .... to solve

حَلّاق (ون/ين) .... barber/hairdresser

حَلّة (حِلَل) .... pot (cooking)

حَلَوِيّات .... sweets

حِمار (حَمير) .... donkey

completely.............................. تَماماً

to sway....................... تَمايَل/يَتَمايَل

statue .... تِمثال (تماثيل)

to hope......................... تَمَنّى/يَتَمَنّى

......................................تَمَهَّلَ/يَتَمَهَّل

to take it easy/slow down ....

variety/variation...............تَنَوُّع (ات)

to renounce, forgo...... تَنازَلَ/يَتَنازَل

breathing...............................تَنَفُّس

digging/excavation................ تَنقيب

congratulations......... تَهنية (تَهاني)

distribution .... تَوزيع

to stop/cease............ تَوَقَّفَ/يَتَوَقَّفَ

agency ....تَوكيل (ات)

ث

wealth/riches .... ثَراء

cultural..................................ثَقافيّ

confidence................................ ثِقة

hard of hearing.............. ثَقيل السَّمع

ice.. ثَلج

body/frame .... جِسم (أجسام)

neighbor....................... جار (جيران)

dry.. جافّ

to dare/venture...............جَرُؤَ/يَجرُؤ

bell..............................جَرَس (أجراس)

newspaper................. جَريدة (جَرائِد)

part/section.................. جُزء (أجزاء)

island............................جَزيرة (جُزُر)

leather/skin..................... جِلد (جُلود)

skull...................... جُمجُمة (جَماجِم)

.... جَمَعَ/يَجمَع

to gather/collect together ....

sentence........................ جُملَة/جُمَل

wing.......................... جَناح (أَجنِحة)

side by side................جَنباً إلى جَنب

system/organization....جِهاز (أجهِزة)

police force....................جِهاز شُرطة

effort ....جَهد (جُهود)

to prepare/make ready....جَهَّزَ/يُجَهِّز

تَخرَّجَ/يَتَخرَّج .... to graduate

تَخزين .... storage

تَخلَّصَ/يَتَخلَّص مِن ...... to get rid of

تَدَفَّقَ/يَتَدَفَّق .... to pour out

تِذكار (ات) .... souvenir

تَذَكَّرَ/يَتَذَكَّر .... to remember

تَذَوَّقَ/يَتَذَوَّق .... to taste

تَراقَصَ/يَتَراقَص .... to dance around

تَربَّى/يَتَربَّى to be brought up/raised

تَرتيب (ات) .... order/arrangement

تَرجَمة .... translation

تَرقِية (ات) .... promotion (job)

تَرَكَ/يَترُك .... to leave (behind)

تَزَوَّجَ/يَتَزَوَّج .... to marry

تَزوير .... forgery

تَسائَلَ/يَتَسائَل .... to wonder

تَسجيل (ات) .... recording

تَسَلَّقَ/يَتَسَلَّق .... to climb

تَسَمَّرَ/يَتَسَمَّر .... to be nailed

تَشابُه (ات) .... likeness/similarity

تَشابَهَ/يَتَشابَه .... to resemble

تَصميم (ات) .... design

تَصوير .... photography

تَعَب .... tiredness

تَعِبَ/يَتعَب (من) .... to tire (of)

تَعَرَّضَ/يَتَعَرَّض .... to be exposed

تَعَطَّلَ/يَتَعَطَّل .... to break down

تَعَلُّم اللُّغات .... learning languages

تَعليمات .... instructions

تَغَيَّرَ/يَتَغَيَّر .... to change

تَغيير (ات) .... change/alteration

تَقدير .... appreciation

تَقشير .... peeling

تَقليديّ .... traditional

تَلّ (تِلال) .... hill

تَلَوُّث .... pollution

تَلاعَبَ/يَتَلاعَب .... to toy with

تَلَعثَمَ/يَتَلَعثَم .... to stutter

تَلَقَّى/يَتَلَقَّى .... to receive

تَمَّ/يَتِمّ .. to be completed/take place

بَرنامَج (بَرامِج) .... program
بَرّيّ .... wild
بَريء .... innocent
بَريق .... sparkle/shine
بُستانيّ (ون/ين) .... gardener
بسيط .... simple
بَصَمات الأَصابِع .... fingerprints
بَضائِع .... goods/products
بَطاطا .... potatoes (sweet)
بَطاقة (ات) .... card (post)
بَطَل (أَبطال) .... hero
بَعدَ فَترة .... after a while
بَعض... .... some of
بَغل (بِغال) .... mule
بَقى/يَبقى .... to stay/remain
بِكلّ سُرور .... with [all] pleasure
بلا .... without
بُنّ .... coffee beans
بِناية (ات) .... building
بُندُق .... hazelnut
بَنَفسَجيّ .... purple
بوق (أَبواق) .... horn (car)

ت

تَأجير السَّيّارات .... car rental
تاريخ .... history, date
تَأشيرة (ات) .... visa
تَأَكُّد .... being sure/certainty
تَأَكَّدَ/يَتَأَكَّد .... to be certain
تائِه .... lost
تاجِر (تُجّار) .... merchant/trader
تَبادَلَ/يَتَبادَل .... to exchange
تَجَوَّلَ/يَتَجَوَّل .... to wander
تَجاهَلَ/يَتَجاهَل .... to ignore
تَحَدَّثَ/يَتَحَدَّث .... to speak/talk
تَحديداً .... specifically
تَحسين (ات) .... improvement
تَحويل (ات) ....
transferring/forwarding (money, etc.)
تَحِيّة (ات) .... greeting
تَخَيَّلَ/يَتَخَيَّل .... to imagine

to finish........................ اِنتَهى/يَنتَهي

achievement.................... إنـجاز (ات)

to found/establish .... أنشَأ/يُنشِئ

to join............................. اِنضَم/يَنضَمّ

nose... أنف

to set off .... اِنطَلَق/يَنطَلِق

to hunch.......................... اِنكَبَّ/يَنكَبّ

to shrink .... اِنكَمَشَ/يَنكَمِش

breaking down/collapsing........ اِنهِيار

elegant .... أنيق

groaning.. أنين

spare/leisure time.......... أوقات الفِراغ

meaning that........................... أيّ أن

receipt........................... إيصال (ات)

ب

gate................................ بـوّابة (ات)

well (water, oil, etc.) .... بِئر (آبار)

to spend the night........... بات/يَبيت

skillful .... بارِع

mosquito........... باعوضة (باعوض)

bouquet............................. باقة (ات)

early (morning)............................. باكِر

precisely................................ بِالتَّحديد

by coincidence...................... بِالصُّدفة

to exaggerate................. بالَغَ/يُبالِغ

wan/thin/pale........................... باهِت

slowly.. بِبُطء

petroleum.................................. بَترول

study/research............... بَحث (أبحاث)

in search of................................ بَحثاً عَن

lake................................... بُحَيرة (ات)

steam.. بُخار

to begin.................................. بَدَأ/يَبدَأ

to seem/appear....................... بَدا/يَبدو

without doubt......................... بِدون شَكّ

Bedouin............................ بَدَويّ (بَدو)

innocence................................... بَراءة

flea....................... برَغوث (بَراغيث)

lightening.................................... بَرق

barrel......................... بَرميل (بَراميل)

preparation.............................. إعداد

trickiest/most complicated....... أعقَد

advertisement................. إعلان (ات)

housework.................. أعمال المَنزِل

most of.................................. أغلَب

songs ....أُغنِية (أَغانٍ)

to approach...........اِقتَرَب/يَقتَرِب مِن

less vibrant......................... أقَلّ بَريقاً

to confirm...........................أَكَّدَ/يُؤَكِّد

For sure!................................ أَكيد!

literature .... الأَدَب

tastiest.. أَلَذّ

the United Nations...... الأُمَم المُتَحِدة

the Pyramids..........................الأَهرام

to gobble......................... اِلتَهَمَ/يَلتَهِم

Algeria .... الجَزائِر

everyone................................ الجَميع

burn(s).................................. الحُروق

four-wheel drive .... الدَّفع الرُّباعيّ

the countryside...................... الريف

politics .... السِّياسة

the police ....الشُّرطة

the Middle East...........الشَرق الأَوسَط

diamonds................................ الماس

Pacific Ocean.............المُحيط الهادئ

more (increase of)............ المَزيد من

architecture.......................... المِعمار

Maghreb/Morocco .... المَغرِب

chaos/pandemonium.. الهَرج والمَرج

machine.............................. آلة (ات)

automated.................................. آليّ

.... اِمتازَ/يَمتاز بِ

to be distinguished/characterized by ..

ideal..أَمثَل

matter/affair..................... أَمر (أُمور)

elegance.................................. أَناقة

to be dazzled ....اِنبَهَر/يَنبَهِر

spread/dissemination .... اِنتِشار

wait(ing).............................. اِنتِظار

to move .... اِنتَقَلَ/يَنتَقِل

widow.......................... أرملة (أَرامِل)

most wonderful.......................... أَروَع

to bother/annoy.............. أَزعَج/يُزعِج

weekly.................................... أُسبوعي

investment................... اِستِثمار (ات)

to use/employ........ اِستَخدَمَ/يَستَخدِم

to rest...................... اِستَراحَ/يَستَريح

اِستَضافَ/يَستَضيف ....

to welcome (as a guest) ....

can/is able to......... اِستَطاعَ/يَستَطيعَ

to prepare.................. اِستَعَدّ/يَستَعِدّ

to last..................... اِستَغرَقَ/يَستَغرِق

to greet/receive...... اِستَقبَلَ/يَستَقبِل

to enjoy.................. اِستَمتَعَ/يستَمتِع

to continue................. اِستَمَرَّ (يَستَمِرّ)

to wake up............... اِستَيقَظَ/يَستَيقِظ

to captivate/capture......... أَسَرَ/يأسِر

family .... أُسرة (أُسَر)

to hurry.......................... أَسرَعَ/يُسرِع

ambulance .... (سَيّارة) إسعاف

sorry.. آسِف

style/method........... أُسلوب (أَساليب)

pyseudonym.................... اسم الشُّهرة

central Asia .... آسيا الوُسطَى

signal/sign....................... إشارة (ات)

subscription.................. اِشتِراك (ات)

to be famous .... اِشتَهَر/يَشتَهِر

to rise (sun).................. أَشرَقَ (يُشرِق)

to occupy/keep busy...... شَغَلَ/يَشغَل

most delicious.......................... أَشهَى

to become................. أَصبَحَ /يُصبِح

to go fishing.. اِصطادَ/يَصطاد السَمَك

native/original......................... أَصليّ

thoroughbred.......................... أَصيل

to overlook................ أَطَلَّ/يُطِلّ على

to relax/not worry...... اِطمَأَنَّ/يَطمَئِنّ

tastiest/best............................ أَطيَب

to consider/think .... اِعتَبَرَ/يعتَبِر

to think/believe............ اِعتَقَدَ/يَعتَقِد

to please.................... أَعجَبَ/يُعجِب

smiling............................... اِبتِسام

to smile............................. اِبتَسَمَ/يَبتَسِم

to swallow.......................... اِبتَلَعَ/يَبتَلِع

alphabetical......................... أَبجَدِيّ

creativity, originality .... إبداع

stupid....................................... أَبلَه

the Sphinx............................ أبو الهول

direction........................... اِتِّجاه (ات)

to head (toward).. اِتَّجَهَ/يَتَّجِه (نَحو)

to widen/become wider.. اِتَّسَعَ/يَتَّسِع

to contact........................... اِتَّصَلَ/يَتَّصِل

to agree.............................. اِتَّفَقَ/يَتَّفِق

command/mastery .... إتقان

ruins, monuments...................... آثار

archeological.............................. أَثَرِيّ

to attract......................... اِجتَذَبَ/يَجتَذِب

fee.. أَجر (أُجور)

to need.............................. اِحتاجَ/يَحتاج

respect .... اِحتِرام

to hug............................ اِحتَضَنَ/يَحتَضِن

to keep........................ اِحتَفَظَ/يَحتَفِظ

the most recent .... أَحدَث

to embarrass.......................... أحرَجَ/يُحرِج

emotion .... إحساس (أحاسيس)

invention........................... اِختِراع (ات)

to invent/make up...... اِختَرَعَ/يَختَرِع

final... أخير

to run/organize..................... أدارَ/يُدير

to perform/carry out........ أَدَّى/يُؤَدّي

literary figure .... أَديب (أُدَباء)

smartest/cleverest......................... أَذكى

ear................................... أُذُن (آذان)

to wear......................... اِرتَدَى/يَرتَدي

to tremble.................... اِرتَعَشَ/يَرتَعِش

to rise.......................... اِرتَفَعَ/يَرتَفِع

have mercy on me............... اِرحَمني

archive.. أَرشيف

terrestrial .... أَرضيّ

to force.......................... أَرغَمَ (يُرغِم)

Glossary

Note that the Arabic–English Glossary runs in the Arabic direction, i.e., from right to left. It starts on page 223 and runs toward the middle of the book until page 200.

The Arabic–English Glossary contains all the key vocabulary in *Easy Arabic Reader* in Arabic alphabetical order for easy reference. You can look up a word in the Glossary if you need to remind yourself of its meaning.

The Glossary and notes next to the main text should give you most of the vocabulary that you need to understand the passages. However, the Glossary does not contain elementary Arabic words that you should be able to recognize; nor does it include alternative meanings not covered in *Easy Arabic Reader*. For these you will need to use a more comprehensive Arabic–English dictionary such as *A Dictionary of Modern Written Arabic* (Hans Wehr).

Note the following:

- The Arabic words are in strict alphabetical order, rather than in order of their root letters.
- Arabic nouns are followed by their plurals in brackets, if appropriate: e.g.,

  island.............................. جَزيرة (جُزُر)

- Arabic verbs are shown in the past tense followed by the present tense and are indicated in English using the infinitive ("to") form: e.g.,

  to think/believe.............. اِعتَقَدَ/ يَعتَقِد